TREASURY OF Holiday COOKIES

PUBLICATIONS INTERNATIONAL, LTD.

Cover photography by Sacco Productions Limited, Chicago

Pictured on the front cover: Kentucky Bourbon Pecan Tarts (*page 73*), Hidden Treasures (*page 26*), Chocolate Pistachio Fingers (*page 72*), Chocolate Raspberry Linzer Cookies (*page 108*), Chocolate-Dipped Almond Horns (*page 16*) and Anise Stars (*page 167*).

Pictured on the opposite page (*top to bottom*): Almond Rice Madeleines (*page 70*); Chocolate Mint Pinwheels (*page 106*), Chocolate Raspberry Linzer Cookies (*page 108*) and New Wave Chocolate Spritz Cookies (*page 108*); Anise Stars (*page 167*), Rum Raisin Balls (*page 167*), Noel Tarts (*page 167*) and Chocolate-Frosted Almond Bars (*page 167*).

ISBN: 0-7853-0791-5

Library of Congress Catalog Card Number: 94-66810

Manufactured in U.S.A.

8 7 6 5 4 3 2 1

Microwave Cooking: Microwave ovens vary in wattage. The cooking times given in this publication are approximate. Use the cooking times as guidelines and check for doneness before adding more time. Consult manufacturer's instructions for suitable microwave-safe cooking dishes.

CONTENTS

INTRODUCTION 4

CHRISTMAS COOKIES 8

Festive Favorites 10
Cookie Cutter Cutouts 30
Heavenly Chocolate 40
Bevy of Bars 48
Fancy Cookies 66

HOMEMADE HOLIDAY COOKIES 82

Holiday Favorites 84
Chips 'n' Chocolate 98
From the Cookie Jar 118
Brownies & Bars 132
Fanciful Cookies 146

FESTIVE HOLIDAY COOKIES 158

Holiday Specialties 160
Cookie Exchanges 174
Creative Cutouts 188
Cookie Jar Classics 204
Brownie & Bar Greats 216

INDEX 234

Introduction

Welcome to the festive world of *Treasury of Holiday Cookies.* We've combined three of our favorite holiday cookie books into one easy-to-use volume to give you hundreds of wonderful recipes, perfect for holiday dessert planning. You will love the versatility and diversity of this cookbook. From the simplest drop cookie to the fanciest chocolate-dipped, if you read the following cookie-baking basics before you begin, you'll be assured perfect results every time.

PREPARATION TIPS

The endless variety of cookies can be divided into five basic types: bar, drop, refrigerator, rolled and shaped. These types are determined by the consistency of the dough and how it is formed into cookies.

Bar Cookies: Bar cookies and brownies are two of the easiest cookies to make—simply mix the batter, spread it in the pan and bake. These cookies are also quick to prepare since they bake all at once rather than in several batches on a cookie sheet.

Always use the pan size specified in the recipe. Substituting a pan of a different size will affect the cookies' cooking time and texture. A smaller pan will cause the bars to become cakelike and a larger pan will produce a flatter bar with a drier texture.

Most bar cookies should cool in the pan set on a wire rack until barely warm before cutting into bars or squares. Try cutting bar cookies into triangles or diamonds for a festive new shape. To make serving easy, remove a corner piece first, then remove the rest.

Sift bar cookies with powdered sugar for a simple garnish. Dress up frosted bar cookies by topping with nuts, chocolate chips or curls, or dried or candied fruit.

Drop Cookies: These cookies are named for the way they are formed. Spoonfuls of soft dough are dropped onto a cookie sheet and flatten during baking. Space the mounds of dough about 2 inches apart on cookie sheets to allow for spreading unless the recipe directs otherwise.

Spoonfuls of dough that are uniform in size and shape will finish baking at the same time. To easily shape drop cookies in a uniform size, use an ice cream scoop with a release bar. The bar usually has a number on it to indicate the number of scoops that can be made from one quart of ice cream. The handiest sizes for cookies are a #80 or #90 scoop. This will yield about one rounded teaspoonful of dough for each cookie.

Refrigerator Cookies: Refrigerator doughs are perfect for advance preparation. Tightly wrapped rolls of dough can be stored in the refrigerator for up to one week or frozen for up to six weeks. These rich doughs are ready to slice and bake at a moment's notice.

Always shape the dough into rolls before chilling. Shaping is easier if you first place the dough on a piece of waxed paper or plastic wrap. If desired, you can gently press chopped nuts, flaked coconut or colored sugar into the roll. Before chilling, wrap the rolls securely in plastic wrap or air may penetrate the dough and cause it to dry out.

Use gentle pressure and a back-and-forth sawing motion when slicing the rolls so the cookies will keep their round shape. Rotating the roll while slicing prevents one side from flattening.

Rolled Cookies: Rolled or cutout cookies are made from stiff doughs that are rolled out and cut into shapes with floured cookie cutters, a knife or a pastry wheel.

Chill the cookie dough before rolling for easier handling. Remove only enough dough from the refrigerator to work with at one time. Collect the trimmings and reroll all at once to prevent the dough from becoming tough.

To make your own custom-designed cookie cutters, cut a simple shape out of clean, heavy cardboard or poster board. Place the cardboard pattern on the rolled out dough and cut around it using a sharp knife.

Shaped Cookies: These cookies can be simply hand-shaped into balls or crescents, forced through a cookie press or pastry bag into more complex shapes or baked in cookie molds.

By using different plates in a cookie press or different tips on a pastry bag, spritz cookies can be formed into many shapes. If your first efforts are not successful, just transfer the dough back to the cookie press or pastry bag and try again. The dough itself can be flavored or tinted with food coloring and the pressed shapes can be decorated with colored sugar or candied fruit before baking.

TIPS FOR STORING COOKIES

Unbaked cookie dough can be refrigerated for up to one week or frozen for up to six weeks. Rolls of dough should be sealed tightly in plastic wrap; other doughs should be stored in airtight containers. Label dough with baking information for convenience. Store soft and crisp cookies separately at room temperature to prevent changes in texture and flavor. Keep soft cookies in airtight containers. If they begin to dry out, add a piece of apple or bread to the container to help retain moisture. Store crisp cookies in containers with loose-fitting lids to prevent moisture buildup. Store cookies with sticky glazes, fragile decorations and icings in single layers between sheets of waxed paper.

As a rule, crisp cookies freeze better than soft, moist cookies. Rich bar cookies are an exception to this rule since they freeze extremely well. Freeze baked cookies in airtight containers for up to six months. Thaw cookies and brownies unwrapped at room temperature. Meringue-based cookies do *not* freeze well and chocolate-dipped cookies will discolor if frozen.

TIPS FOR SENDING COOKIES

Bake soft, moist cookies that can handle jostling rather than fragile, brittle cookies that might crumble. Brownies and bar cookies are generally sturdy, but avoid shipping those with moist fillings and frostings since they become sticky at room temperature. For the same reason, shipping anything with chocolate during the summer or to warm climates is also risky.

Wrap each type of cookie separately to retain flavors and textures. Cookies can also be wrapped back-to-back in pairs with either plastic wrap or foil. Bar cookies should be packed in layers the size of the container or they can be sent in a covered foil pan as long as the pan is well-cushioned inside the shipping box. Place wrapped cookies as tightly as possible in snug rows inside a sturdy shipping box or container.

Fill the bottom of the shipping container with an even layer of packing material. Do not use popped popcorn or puffed cereal as it may attract insects. Place crumpled waxed paper, newspaper or paper towels between layers of wrapped cookies. Fill any crevices with packing material and add a final layer at the top of the box. Ship the container to arrive as soon as possible.

TOASTING NUTS

Spread the nuts in a single layer on a rimmed baking sheet. Bake in a 325°F oven for 8 to 10 minutes or until golden. Shake the pan or stir the nuts occasionally during baking to ensure even toasting. The nuts will darken and become crisper as they cool. To toast a small amount of nuts, place them in a dry skillet over low heat. Stir constantly for 2 to 4 minutes until the nuts darken slightly.

TOASTING COCONUT

Spread the flaked coconut in a thin layer on a rimmed baking sheet. Bake in a 325°F oven for 7 to 10 minutes. Shake the pan occasionally during baking to promote even browning and prevent burning.

WEIGHTS AND MEASURES

Dash = less than ⅛ teaspoon

½ tablespoon = 1½ teaspoons

1 tablespoon = 3 teaspoons

2 tablespoons = ⅛ cup

¼ cup = 4 tablespoons

⅓ cup = 5 tablespoons plus 1 teaspoon

½ cup = 8 tablespoons

¾ cup = 12 tablespoons

1 cup = 16 tablespoons

½ pint = 1 cup or 8 fluid ounces

1 pint = 2 cups or 16 fluid ounces

1 quart = 4 cups or 2 pints or 32 fluid ounces

1 gallon = 16 cups or 4 quarts

1 pound = 16 ounces

SUBSTITUTION LIST

If you don't have:	**Use:**
1 teaspoon baking powder	¼ teaspoon baking soda + ½ teaspoon cream of tartar
½ cup firmly packed brown sugar	½ cup granulated sugar with 2 tablespoons molasses
1 cup buttermilk	1 tablespoon lemon juice or vinegar plus milk to equal 1 cup (Stir; let mixture stand 5 minutes.)
1 ounce (1 square) unsweetened baking chocolate	3 tablespoons unsweetened cocoa + 1 tablespoon shortening
3 ounces (3 squares) semisweet baking chocolate	3 ounces (½ cup) semisweet chocolate morsels
½ cup corn syrup	½ cup granulated sugar + 2 tablespoons liquid
1 whole egg	2 egg yolks + 1 tablespoon water
1 cup honey	1¼ cups granulated sugar + ¼ cup water
1 teaspoon freshly grated orange or lemon peel	½ teaspoon dried peel

EQUIVALENTS

Almonds, blanched, slivered	4 ounces = 1 cup
Apples	1 medium = 1 cup sliced
Bananas	1 medium, mashed = ⅓ cup
Butter or margarine	2 cups = 1 pound or 4 sticks 1 cup = ½ pound or 2 sticks ½ cup = 1 stick or 8 tablespoons ¼ cup = ½ stick or 4 tablespoons
Chocolate	1 (6-ounce) package chocolate chips = 1 cup chips or 6 (1-ounce) squares semisweet chocolate
Cocoa, unsweetened	1 (8-ounce) can = 2 cups
Coconut, flaked	3½ ounces = 1⅓ cups
Cream cheese	3-ounce package = 6 tablespoons 8-ounce package = 1 cup

Flour
    White or all-purpose
    Whole wheat
	
	1 pound = 3½ to 4 cups
	1 pound = 3¾ to 4 cups

Honey, liquid	16 ounces = 1⅓ cups
Lemons	1 medium = 1 to 3 tablespoons juice and 2 to 3 teaspoons grated peel
Marshmallows	1 cup cut-up = 16 large or 160 miniature

Milk
    Evaporated
 	
    Sweetened, condensed
	
	5-ounce can = ⅝ cup
	12-ounce can = 1½ cups
	14-ounce can = 1¼ cups

Oranges	1 medium = 6 to 8 tablespoons juice and 2 to 3 teaspoons grated peel
Pecans, shelled	1 pound = 4 cups halved and 3½ to 4 cups chopped
Raisins, seedless, whole	1 pound = 2¾ to 3 cups
Shortening	1 pound = 2½ cups

Sugar
    Granulated
    Brown, packed
    Confectioners' or powdered
	
	1 pound = 2½ cups
	1 pound = 2¼ cups
	1 pound = 3¾ to 4 cups, unsifted

Walnuts, chopped	4½ ounces = 1 cup

Almond Rice Madeleines (page 70)

CHRISTMAS COOKIES

Festive Favorites   *10*

Cookie Cutter Cutouts   *30*

Heavenly Chocolate   *40*

Bevy of Bars   *48*

Fancy Cookies   *66*

Festive Favorites

These cookies are sure to bring back delightful holiday memories. Make a batch and start a holiday tradition for your family.

CHOCO–COCO PECAN CRISPS

½ cup butter or margarine, softened
1 cup packed light brown sugar
1 egg
1 teaspoon vanilla
1½ cups all-purpose flour

1 cup chopped pecans
⅓ cup unsweetened cocoa
½ teaspoon baking soda
1 cup flaked coconut

Cream butter and sugar in large bowl until light and fluffy. Beat in egg and vanilla. Combine flour, pecans, cocoa and baking soda in small bowl until well blended. Add to creamed mixture, blending until stiff dough is formed. Sprinkle coconut on work surface. Divide dough into 4 parts. Shape each part into a roll, about 1½ inches in diameter; roll in coconut until thickly coated. Wrap in plastic wrap; chill until firm, at least 1 hour or up to 2 weeks. (For longer storage, freeze up to 6 weeks.)

Preheat oven to 350°F. Line cookie sheets with parchment paper or leave ungreased. Cut rolls into ⅛-inch-thick slices. Place 2 inches apart on cookie sheets.

Bake 10 to 13 minutes or until firm, but not overly browned. Remove to wire racks to cool.

Makes about 6 dozen cookies

Left to right: Choco-Coco Pecan Crisps; Holiday Fruit Drops (page 12)

HOLIDAY FRUIT DROPS

½ cup butter, softened
¾ cup packed brown sugar
1 egg
1¼ cups all-purpose flour
1 teaspoon vanilla
½ teaspoon baking soda
½ teaspoon ground cinnamon
   Pinch salt
1 cup (8 ounces) diced candied
   pineapple

1 cup (8 ounces) red and green
   candied cherries
8 ounces chopped pitted dates
1 cup (6 ounces) semisweet
   chocolate chips
½ cup whole hazelnuts
½ cup pecan halves
½ cup coarsely chopped walnuts

Preheat oven to 325°F. Lightly grease cookie sheets or line with parchment paper. Beat butter and sugar in large bowl. Beat in egg until light and fluffy. Mix in flour, vanilla, baking soda, cinnamon and salt. Stir in pineapple, cherries, dates, chocolate chips, hazelnuts, pecans and walnuts. Drop dough by rounded teaspoonfuls 2 inches apart onto prepared cookie sheets.

Bake 15 to 20 minutes or until firm and lightly browned around edges. Remove to wire racks to cool completely.

Makes about 8 dozen cookies

Note: The cherries, hazelnuts and pecan halves are not chopped, but left whole.

HONEY–GINGER BOURBON BALLS

1 cup gingersnap cookie crumbs
1¼ cups powdered sugar, divided
1 cup finely chopped pecans or
   walnuts

1 square (1 ounce) unsweetened
   chocolate, chopped
1½ tablespoons honey
¼ cup bourbon

Combine crumbs, 1 cup sugar and nuts in large bowl. Combine chocolate and honey in small bowl over hot water; stir until chocolate is melted. Blend in bourbon. Stir bourbon mixture into crumb mixture until well blended. Shape into 1-inch balls. Sprinkle remaining powdered sugar over balls. Refrigerate until firm.

Makes about 4 dozen balls

Note: These improve with aging; store in airtight container in refrigerator. They will keep several weeks, but are best after 2 to 3 days.

LEMON BLOSSOM COOKIES

2 cups margarine or butter, softened
1½ cups confectioners' sugar
¼ cup REALEMON® Lemon Juice from
    Concentrate

4 cups unsifted all-purpose flour
Finely chopped nuts (optional)
Assorted fruit preserves and jams
    or pecan halves

In large mixer bowl, beat margarine and sugar until fluffy. Add ReaLemon® brand; beat well. Gradually add flour; mix well. Cover and chill 2 hours.

Preheat oven to 350°F. Grease cookie sheets. Shape dough into 1-inch balls; roll in nuts, if desired. Place 1 inch apart on prepared cookie sheets. Press thumb in center of each ball; fill with preserves or pecan half.

Bake 14 to 16 minutes or until lightly browned. Remove to wire racks to cool completely.

Makes about 6 dozen cookies

EUROPEAN KOLACKY

1 cup butter or margarine, softened
1 package (8 ounces) cream cheese,
    softened
1 tablespoon milk
1 tablespoon sugar
1 egg yolk

1½ cups all-purpose flour
½ teaspoon baking powder
1 can SOLO® or 1 jar BAKER® Filling
    (any flavor)
Confectioners' sugar

Beat butter, cream cheese, milk and sugar in medium bowl with electric mixer until thoroughly blended. Beat in egg yolk. Sift together flour and baking powder; stir into butter mixture to make stiff dough. Cover and refrigerate several hours or overnight.

Preheat oven to 400°F. Roll out dough on lightly floured surface to ¼-inch thickness. Cut dough with floured 2-inch cookie cutter. Place cookies on ungreased cookie sheets about 1 inch apart. Make depression in centers of cookies with thumb or back of spoon. Spoon 1 teaspoon filling into centers of cookies.

Bake 10 to 12 minutes or until lightly browned. Remove from baking sheets and cool completely on wire racks. Sprinkle with confectioners' sugar just before serving. *Makes about 3 dozen cookies*

APRICOT–PECAN TASSIES

BASE
1 cup all-purpose flour
½ cup butter, cut into pieces

6 tablespoons reduced calorie cream cheese

FILLING
¾ cup firmly packed light brown sugar
1 egg, lightly beaten
1 tablespoon butter, softened
½ teaspoon vanilla

¼ teaspoon salt
⅔ cup California dried apricot halves, diced (about 4 ounces)
⅓ cup chopped pecans

For base, in food processor, combine flour, ½ cup butter and cream cheese; process until mixture forms large ball. Wrap dough in plastic wrap and chill 15 minutes.

For filling, combine brown sugar, egg, 1 tablespoon butter, vanilla and salt in bowl until smooth. Stir in apricots and nuts.

Preheat oven to 325°F. Shape dough into 2 dozen 1-inch balls and place in paper-lined or greased miniature muffin cups. Press dough on bottom and up side of each cup; fill each with 1 teaspoon apricot-pecan filling. Bake 25 minutes or until golden and filling sets. Cool and remove from cups. Cookies can be wrapped tightly in plastic and frozen up to six weeks.   *Makes 2 dozen cookies*

Favorite recipe from California Apricot Advisory Board

SNOWBALLS

½ cup DOMINO® Confectioners 10-X Sugar
¼ teaspoon salt
1 cup butter or margarine, softened
1 teaspoon vanilla extract

2¼ cups all-purpose flour
½ cup chopped pecans
Additional DOMINO® Confectioners 10-X Sugar

In large bowl, combine ½ cup sugar, salt and butter; mix well. Add vanilla. Gradually stir in flour. Mix nuts into dough. Cover and chill until firm.

Preheat oven to 400°F. Form dough into 1-inch balls. Place 1 inch apart on ungreased cookie sheets. Bake 8 to 10 minutes or until set, but not brown. Roll in additional sugar immediately. Cool on wire racks. Roll in sugar again. Store in airtight container.   *Makes about 5 dozen cookies*

Apricot-Pecan Tassies

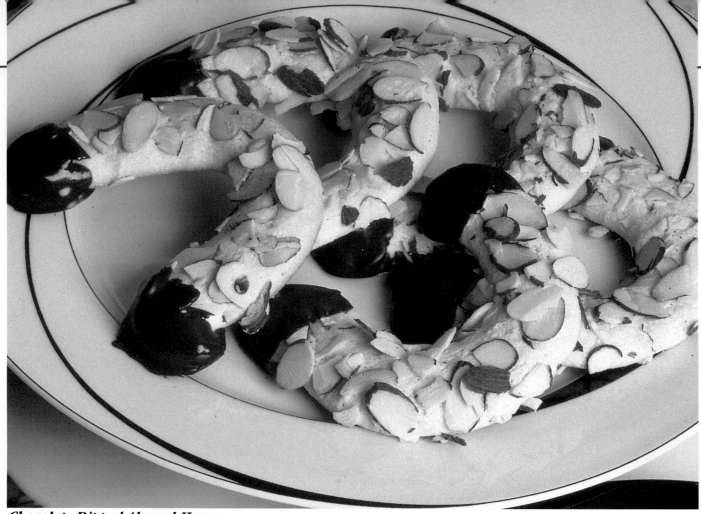

Chocolate-Dipped Almond Horns

CHOCOLATE–DIPPED ALMOND HORNS

1 can SOLO® Almond Paste
3 egg whites
½ cup superfine sugar
½ teaspoon almond extract
¼ cup plus 2 tablespoons all-purpose
    flour

½ cup sliced almonds
5 squares (1 ounce each) semisweet
    chocolate, melted and cooled

Preheat oven to 350°F. Grease 2 cookie sheets; set aside. Break almond paste into small pieces and place in medium bowl or container of food processor. Add egg whites, sugar and almond extract. Beat with electric mixer or process until mixture is very smooth. Add flour and beat or process until blended. Spoon almond mixture into pastry bag fitted with ½-inch (#8) plain tip. Pipe mixture into 5- or 6-inch crescent shapes on prepared cookie sheets about 1½ inches apart. Sprinkle with sliced almonds.

Bake 13 to 15 minutes or until edges are golden. Cool on cookie sheets on wire racks 2 minutes. Remove from cookie sheets and cool completely on wire racks. Dip ends of cookies in melted chocolate and place on sheet of foil. Let stand until chocolate is set. *Makes about 16 cookies*

SPRITZ COOKIES

1¼ cups granulated sugar
1 cup BUTTER FLAVOR* CRISCO®
   All-Vegetable Shortening
2 eggs
¼ cup light corn syrup or regular
   pancake syrup

1 teaspoon vanilla
1 teaspoon almond extract
3 cups all-purpose flour
¾ teaspoon baking powder
½ teaspoon baking soda
½ teaspoon salt

1. Heat oven to 375°F.

2. Combine sugar and shortening in large bowl. Beat at medium speed of electric mixer until light and fluffy. Add eggs, corn syrup, vanilla and almond extract. Beat until well blended and fluffy.

3. Combine flour, baking powder, baking soda and salt in large bowl. Add gradually to shortening mixture at low speed. Mix until well blended. Fill cookie press or pastry bag with dough, following manufacturer's directions. Press dough out 2 inches apart onto cold baking sheets. Decorate as desired.

4. Bake one sheet at a time at 375°F for 7 to 9 minutes or until bottoms are golden. Cool 2 minutes on baking sheet. Remove to wire rack to cool completely.   *Makes about 7 to 8 dozen cookies*

*BUTTER FLAVOR CRISCO® is artificially flavored.

ALMOND RASPBERRY MACAROONS

Macaroons are a classic favorite. Here, the deliciously intense flavor of almond paste is punctuated by a dot of raspberry jam.

2 cups BLUE DIAMOND® Blanched
   Almond Paste
1 cup granulated sugar
6 large egg whites

Powdered sugar
Seedless raspberry jam, stirred
   until smooth

Preheat oven to 350°F. Line cookie sheets with parchment paper or waxed paper. Beat almond paste and granulated sugar until mixture resembles coarse cornmeal. Beat in egg whites, a little at a time, until thoroughly combined.

Place heaping teaspoonfuls 2 inches apart onto prepared cookie sheets. Coat finger with powdered sugar and make an indentation in middle of each cookie. (Coat finger with powdered sugar each time.)

Bake 15 to 20 minutes or until lightly browned. Remove from oven and fill each indentation with about ¼ teaspoon raspberry jam. Cool. If using waxed paper, carefully peel paper off cookies when cooled.
          Makes about 2½ dozen cookies

LEMONY SPRITZ STICKS

1 cup margarine or butter, softened
1 cup confectioners' sugar
¼ cup REALEMON® Lemon Juice from
    Concentrate

2½ cups unsifted all-purpose flour
¼ teaspoon salt
Chocolate Glaze (recipe follows)
Finely chopped nuts

Preheat oven to 375°F. Grease cookie sheets. In large bowl, beat margarine and sugar until fluffy. Add ReaLemon® brand; beat well. Stir in flour and salt; mix well.

Place dough in cookie press with star-shaped plate. Press dough into 3-inch strips onto prepared cookie sheets. Bake 5 to 6 minutes or until lightly browned on ends. Cool 1 to 2 minutes on cookie sheets. Remove to wire racks to cool completely. Prepare Chocolate Glaze. Dip ends of cookies in glaze, then nuts.   *Makes about 8½ dozen cookies*

Tip: When using electric cookie gun, use decorator tip. Press dough into ½ × 3-inch strips onto greased cookie sheets. Bake 8 to 10 minutes or until lightly browned on ends.

Chocolate Glaze: In small saucepan, melt 3 ounces sweet cooking chocolate and 2 tablespoons margarine or butter.   *Makes about ⅓ cup*

SLICE 'N' BAKE PUMPKIN COOKIES

3 cups all-purpose flour
1 tablespoon pumpkin pie spice
2 teaspoons ground ginger
½ teaspoon salt

1 cup butter, softened
2 cups granulated sugar
1 cup LIBBY'S® Solid Pack Pumpkin
1 egg yolk

In medium bowl, combine flour, pumpkin pie spice, ginger and salt; set aside. In large mixer bowl, beat butter and sugar until light and fluffy. Add pumpkin and egg yolk; mix well. Blend in dry ingredients; mix well. Cover and chill until firm. Divide into 4 parts. Place each part on 14×10-inch sheet of plastic wrap. Wrap loosely around dough. Shape into 1½-inch-diameter roll; wrap securely. Freeze 4 hours or until firm.

Preheat oven to 350°F. Grease cookie sheets. Cut rolls into ¼-inch slices. Place 2 inches apart on prepared cookie sheets; pat to spread slightly. Reserve some slices to make pumpkin stems; cut into fourths. Shape and press onto tops of cookie slices to form stems.

Bake 16 to 18 minutes or until lightly browned. Remove to wire racks to cool completely. Decorate in pumpkin design with orange and green frosting, if desired.   *Makes about 5 dozen cookies*

Hint: Spread orange frosting with small spatula. Pipe leaves using leaf frosting tip, then vines with smallest frosting tip.

BAVARIAN COOKIE WREATHS

Use various decorations for special holidays—or serve plain.

3½ cups all-purpose flour
1 cup sugar, divided
3 teaspoons grated orange peel,
   divided
¼ teaspoon salt
1⅓ cups butter or margarine

¼ cup Florida orange juice
⅓ cup finely chopped blanched
   almonds
1 egg white beaten *with* 1 teaspoon
   water
Tinted Frosting (recipe follows)

Preheat oven to 400°F. Lightly grease cookie sheets. In large bowl, mix flour, ¾ cup sugar, 2 teaspoons orange peel and salt. Using pastry blender, cut in butter until mixture resembles coarse crumbs; add orange juice, stirring until mixture holds together. Knead a few times and press into a ball.

Shape dough into ¾-inch balls; lightly roll each on floured surface into 6-inch-long strip. Using two strips, twist together to make rope. Pinch ends of rope together to make wreath; place on prepared cookie sheets.

In shallow dish, mix almonds, remaining ¼ cup sugar and 1 teaspoon orange peel. Brush top of wreaths with egg white mixture and sprinkle with almond-sugar mixture. Bake 8 to 10 minutes or until lightly browned. Remove to wire racks to cool completely. Frost, if desired.   *Makes about 5 dozen cookies*

TINTED FROSTING

1 cup confectioners' sugar
2 tablespoons butter or margarine,
   softened

1 to 2 teaspoons milk
Few drops green food color
Red cinnamon candies

In small bowl, mix sugar, butter, 1 teaspoon milk and few drops green food color. Add more milk if necessary to make frosting spreadable. Fill pastry bag fitted with small leaf tip (#67). Decorate each wreath with 3 or 4 leaves and red-cinnamon-candy berries.

Favorite recipe from Florida Department of Citrus

PEANUT BUTTER CHOCOLATE BARS

½ cup (1 stick) margarine, softened
⅓ cup sugar
½ cup QUAKER® or AUNT JEMIMA®
    Enriched Corn Meal
½ cup all-purpose flour

½ cup chopped almonds
½ cup peanut butter
¼ cup semisweet chocolate pieces
1 teaspoon shortening

Preheat oven to 375°F. Beat margarine and sugar in medium bowl until light and fluffy. Stir in corn meal, flour and almonds. Press onto bottom of ungreased 9-inch square baking pan.

Bake 25 to 30 minutes or until edges are light golden brown. Cool about 10 minutes; spread with peanut butter. In saucepan over low heat, melt chocolate pieces and shortening, stirring until smooth.* Drizzle over peanut butter. Cool completely in pan on wire rack. Cut into bars. Store tightly covered.

Makes 16 bars

Microwave directions: Place chocolate pieces and shortening in microwaveable bowl. Microwave at HIGH (100% power) 1 to 1½ minutes, stirring after 1 minute and then every 15 seconds until smooth.

HERSHEY®'S CHOCOLATE CHIP BLONDIES

¾ cup packed light brown sugar
6 tablespoons butter or margarine,
    softened
1 egg
1 tablespoon milk
1 teaspoon vanilla extract
1 cup all-purpose flour

½ teaspoon baking soda
⅛ teaspoon salt
2 cups (12-ounce package)
    HERSHEY®'S Semi-Sweet
    Chocolate Chips
½ cup coarsely chopped nuts
    (optional)

Preheat oven to 350°F. Grease 9-inch square baking pan. In large mixer bowl, beat brown sugar and butter until light and fluffy. Add egg, milk and vanilla; beat well. Stir together flour, baking soda and salt; add to butter mixture. Stir in chocolate chips and nuts, if desired; spread in prepared pan. Bake 20 to 25 minutes or until lightly browned. Cool completely in pan on wire rack. Cut into bars.

Makes about 1½ dozen bars

CRISPY NUT SHORTBREAD

6 tablespoons margarine, softened
⅓ cup sugar
1 egg
1 teaspoon vanilla
½ cup QUAKER® or AUNT JEMIMA®
    Enriched Corn Meal

½ cup all-purpose flour
½ cup finely chopped, husked,
    toasted hazelnuts or walnuts
½ cup semisweet chocolate pieces
1 tablespoon vegetable shortening
Coarsely chopped nuts (optional)

Preheat oven to 300°F. Grease 13×9-inch baking pan. Beat margarine and sugar until fluffy. Blend in egg and vanilla. Add combined corn meal, flour and ½ cup nuts; mix well. Spread onto bottom of prepared pan. Bake 40 to 45 minutes or until edges are golden brown.

In saucepan over low heat, melt chocolate pieces and shortening, stirring until smooth.* Spread over shortbread. Sprinkle with coarsely chopped nuts, if desired. Cool completely. Cut into 48 squares; cut diagonally into triangles. Store tightly covered. *Makes 8 dozen cookies*

*Microwave directions: Place chocolate pieces and shortening in microwaveable bowl. Microwave at HIGH (100% power) 1 to 2 minutes, stirring after 1 minute and then every 30 seconds until smooth.

Peanut Butter Chocolate Bars; Crispy Nut Shortbread

PEANUT BUTTER CRACKLES

1½ cups all-purpose flour
1 teaspoon baking soda
⅛ teaspoon salt
½ cup MAZOLA® Margarine, softened
½ cup SKIPPY® Creamy or Super
   Chunk Peanut Butter

½ cup granulated sugar
½ cup packed brown sugar
1 egg
1 teaspoon vanilla
   Granulated sugar
   Chocolate candy stars

Preheat oven to 375°F. In small bowl, combine flour, baking soda and salt. In large bowl, beat margarine and peanut butter until well blended. Beat in ½ cup granulated sugar and brown sugar until blended. Beat in egg and vanilla. Gradually beat in flour mixture until well mixed.

Shape dough into 1-inch balls. Roll in granulated sugar. Place 2 inches apart on ungreased cookie sheets.

Bake 10 minutes or until lightly browned. Remove from oven and quickly press chocolate star firmly into top of each cookie (cookie will crack around edges). Remove to wire racks to cool completely.

Makes about 5 dozen cookies

JINGLE JUMBLES

¾ cup butter or margarine, softened
1 cup packed brown sugar
¼ cup molasses
1 egg
2¼ cups unsifted all-purpose flour
2 teaspoons baking soda

1 teaspoon ground ginger
1 teaspoon ground cinnamon
½ teaspoon salt
½ teaspoon ground cloves
1¼ cups SUN•MAID® Raisins
   Granulated sugar

In large bowl, beat butter and brown sugar. Add molasses and egg; beat until fluffy. In medium bowl, sift together flour, baking soda, ginger, cinnamon, salt and cloves. Stir into molasses mixture. Stir in raisins. Cover and chill about 30 minutes.

Preheat oven to 375°F. Grease cookie sheets. Form dough into 1½-inch balls; roll in granulated sugar, coating generously. Place 2 inches apart on prepared cookie sheets.

Bake 12 to 14 minutes or until edges are firm and centers are still slightly soft. Remove to wire racks to cool.

Makes about 2 dozen cookies

Holiday Citrus Log

HOLIDAY CITRUS LOGS

1 (12-ounce) package vanilla wafers, crushed (about 3 cups)

1 (8-ounce) package candied cherries, coarsely chopped

1 (8-ounce) package chopped dates (1¾ cups)

1 cup chopped pecans or almonds

¼ cup REALEMON® Lemon Juice from Concentrate

2 tablespoons orange-flavored liqueur

1 tablespoon white corn syrup

Additional white corn syrup, heated

Additional finely chopped pecans or sliced almonds, toasted

In large bowl, combine all ingredients except additional corn syrup and finely chopped nuts. Shape into two 10-inch logs. Brush with additional corn syrup; roll in finely chopped nuts. Wrap tightly; refrigerate 3 to 4 days to blend flavors. To serve, cut into ¼-inch slices.   *Makes 2 (10-inch) logs*

MERRY CHERRY MACAROONS

3 egg whites
¼ teaspoon cream of tartar
½ cup sugar
½ teaspoon vanilla

½ teaspoon almond extract
1⅓ cups (3½ ounces) flaked coconut
½ cup chopped red glacé cherries
Red glacé cherry halves (optional)

Preheat oven to 325°F. Grease cookie sheets or line with foil, waxed paper or parchment paper. In small bowl, beat egg whites and cream of tartar at high speed of electric mixer until foamy. Add sugar, 1 tablespoon at a time, beating constantly until sugar is dissolved* and whites are glossy and stand in soft peaks. Beat in flavorings. Stir together coconut and chopped cherries. Gently, but thoroughly, fold into beaten whites. Drop by rounded tablespoonfuls 2 inches apart onto prepared cookie sheets. Top each cookie with cherry half, if desired.

Bake 18 to 20 minutes until lightly browned. Remove to wire racks to cool completely. Store in airtight container between sheets of foil or waxed paper.   *Makes 3½ to 4 dozen cookies*

*Rub a bit of meringue between fingers to feel if sugar has dissolved.

Favorite recipe from American Egg Board

LEMON WAFERS

¾ cup (1½ sticks) margarine,
   softened
½ cup sugar
1 egg
1 tablespoon grated lemon peel
   (about 1 medium lemon)

2 cups QUAKER® or AUNT JEMIMA®
   Enriched Corn Meal
1½ cups all-purpose flour
½ teaspoon salt (optional)
¼ cup milk

Preheat oven to 375°F. Beat margarine and sugar until fluffy. Blend in egg and lemon peel. Add combined dry ingredients alternately with milk, mixing well after each addition.

Shape into 1-inch balls. Place 2 inches apart on ungreased cookie sheets. Using bottom of greased glass dipped in sugar, press into ⅛-inch-thick circles. Bake 13 to 15 minutes or until bottoms are lightly browned. Cool 2 minutes on cookie sheets; remove to wire racks. Cool completely. Store tightly covered.   *Makes about 3 dozen cookies*

ISLAND TREASURE COOKIES

1⅔ cups all-purpose flour
¾ teaspoon baking powder
½ teaspoon baking soda
½ teaspoon salt
14 tablespoons (1¾ sticks) butter,
    softened
¾ cup firmly packed brown sugar
⅓ cup granulated sugar

1 teaspoon vanilla extract
1 egg
¾ cup coconut, toasted if desired
¾ cup macadamia nuts or walnuts,
    chopped
2 cups (12-ounce package) NESTLÉ®
    Toll House® Milk Chocolate
    Morsels

Preheat oven to 375°F. In small bowl, combine flour, baking powder, baking soda and salt; set aside.

In large mixer bowl, beat butter, brown sugar, granulated sugar and vanilla extract until creamy. Beat in egg. Gradually blend in flour mixture. Stir in coconut, nuts and morsels. Drop by slightly rounded measuring tablespoonfuls onto ungreased cookie sheets.

Bake 10 to 12 minutes until edges are lightly browned. Let stand 2 minutes. Remove from cookie sheets; cool.   *Makes about 2 dozen cookies*

DOUBLE ALMOND BUTTER COOKIES

2 cups butter or margarine, softened
2½ cups powdered sugar, sifted and
    divided
4 cups all-purpose flour
2¼ teaspoons vanilla, divided
⅔ cup BLUE DIAMOND® Blanched
    Almond Paste

½ cup BLUE DIAMOND® Chopped
    Natural Almonds, toasted
¼ cup firmly packed light brown
    sugar

Beat butter with 1 cup powdered sugar in large bowl until light and fluffy. Gradually beat in flour. Beat in 2 teaspoons of the vanilla. Cover and chill 30 minutes.

Preheat oven to 350°F. Combine almond paste, almonds, brown sugar and remaining ¼ teaspoon vanilla. Shape dough around ½ teaspoon almond paste mixture; form into 1-inch balls. Place on ungreased cookie sheets.

Bake 15 minutes or until set. Remove to wire racks to cool. Roll in remaining 1½ cups powdered sugar or sift powdered sugar over cookies.   *Makes about 8 dozen cookies*

HIDDEN TREASURES

COOKIES
⅔ **cup granulated sugar**
½ **cup BUTTER FLAVOR* CRISCO®**
All-Vegetable Shortening
1 **egg**
2 **tablespoons light corn syrup or**
regular pancake syrup
1 **teaspoon vanilla**

1¾ **cups all-purpose flour**
½ **teaspoon baking powder**
¼ **teaspoon baking soda**
¼ **teaspoon salt**
48 **maraschino cherries, well drained**
on paper towels

WHITE DIPPING CHOCOLATE
1 **cup white melting chocolate, cut in**
small pieces

2 **tablespoons BUTTER FLAVOR***
CRISCO® All-Vegetable
Shortening

DARK DIPPING CHOCOLATE
1 **cup semisweet chocolate chips**

2 **tablespoons BUTTER FLAVOR***
CRISCO® All-Vegetable
Shortening

Finely chopped pecans

Slivered white chocolate

1. Heat oven to 350°F.

2. **For cookies,** combine sugar and ½ cup shortening in large bowl. Beat at medium speed of electric mixer until well blended. Add egg, corn syrup and vanilla. Beat until light and fluffy. Combine flour, baking powder, baking soda and salt in small bowl. Add gradually to shortening mixture at low speed. Mix until well blended. Divide dough into 48 equal pieces.

3. Press dough into very thin layer around well-drained cherries. Place 2 inches apart on ungreased baking sheets. Bake at 350°F for 10 minutes. Cool 2 minutes on baking sheets. Remove to wire racks to cool completely.

4. **For dipping chocolate,** place chocolate of choice and 2 tablespoons shortening in glass measuring cup. Microwave at MEDIUM (50% power). Stir after 1 minute. Repeat until smooth (or melt on range top in small saucepan on very low heat). Drop one cookie at a time into chocolate. Use fork to turn. Cover completely with chocolate. Lift cookie out of chocolate with fork. Allow excess to drip off. Place on waxed paper-lined baking sheet.

5. Sprinkle chopped pecans on top of white chocolate cookies before chocolate sets. Sprinkle white chocolate slivers on dark chocolate cookies before chocolate sets. Chill in refrigerator to set chocolate.

Makes 4 dozen cookies

*BUTTER FLAVOR CRISCO® is artificially flavored.

HOLIDAY CHOCOLATE CHIP COOKIES

2¼ cups all-purpose flour
1¼ teaspoons baking powder
¼ teaspoon salt
1 cup (2 sticks) butter, softened
1¼ cups sugar
1 egg
1 teaspoon vanilla extract
2 cups (12-ounce package) NESTLÉ®
   Toll House® Semi-Sweet
   Chocolate Morsels

1 cup chopped nuts
3 jars (6 ounces each) maraschino
   cherries, drained, patted dry
8 small candy spearmint leaves, cut
   into quarters lengthwise and
   halved

Preheat oven to 350°F. In small bowl, combine flour, baking powder and salt; set aside.

In large mixer bowl, beat butter and sugar until creamy. Beat in egg and vanilla extract. Gradually blend in flour mixture. Stir in morsels and nuts. Spread in greased 13×9-inch baking pan. Press 30 maraschino cherries into dough, spacing them to form 6 rows, 5 cherries per row. Place 2 spearmint ''leaves'' at base of each cherry; press into dough.

Bake 25 to 30 minutes. Cool completely. Cut into 2-inch squares.   *Makes 30 cookies*

Hidden Treasures

Walnut Christmas Balls

WALNUT CHRISTMAS BALLS

1 cup California walnuts
⅔ cup powdered sugar, divided
1 cup butter or margarine, softened

1 teaspoon vanilla
1¾ cups all-purpose flour
Chocolate Filling (recipe follows)

Preheat oven to 350°F. In food processor or blender, process walnuts with 2 tablespoons of the sugar until finely ground; set aside. In large bowl, beat butter and remaining sugar. Beat in vanilla. Add flour and ¾ cup of the ground walnuts; mix until blended. Roll dough into about 3 dozen walnut-size balls. Place 2 inches apart on ungreased cookie sheets.

Bake 10 to 12 minutes or until just golden around edges. Remove to wire racks to cool completely.

Prepare Chocolate Filling. Place generous teaspoonful of filling on flat side of half of the cookies. Top with remaining cookies, flat side down, forming sandwiches. Roll chocolate edges of cookies in remaining ground walnuts.   *Makes about 1½ dozen sandwich cookies*

Chocolate Filling: Chop 3 squares (1 ounce each) semisweet chocolate into small pieces; place in food processor or blender with ½ teaspoon vanilla. In small saucepan, heat 2 tablespoons each butter or margarine and whipping cream over medium heat until hot; pour over chocolate. Process until chocolate is melted, turning machine off and scraping side as needed. With machine running, gradually add 1 cup powdered sugar; process until smooth.

Favorite recipe from Walnut Marketing Board

"M&M'S"® CHOCOLATE CANDIES EASY PARTY COOKIES

1 cup butter or margarine, softened
1 cup packed light brown sugar
½ cup granulated sugar
2 eggs
2 teaspoons vanilla

2¼ cups all-purpose flour
1 teaspoon salt
1 teaspoon baking soda
1½ cups "M&M'S"® Plain Chocolate
Candies, divided

Preheat oven to 375°F. Beat together butter, brown sugar and granulated sugar in large bowl until light and fluffy. Blend in eggs and vanilla. Combine flour, salt and baking soda in small bowl. Add to butter mixture; mix well. Stir in ½ cup of the candies. Drop dough by rounded teaspoonfuls 2 inches apart onto ungreased cookie sheets. Press additional candies into each cookie. Bake 10 to 12 minutes or until golden brown. Remove to wire racks to cool completely.   *Makes about 6 dozen cookies*

Cookie Cutter Cutouts

Decorating cutout cookies is great fun for the family. Use frostings, colored sugars, candied fruit, chopped nuts, small candies and your imagination.

PEANUT BUTTER CUTOUT COOKIES

1 cup REESE'S® Peanut Butter Chips
½ cup butter or margarine
⅔ cup packed light brown sugar
1 egg
¾ teaspoon vanilla extract

1⅓ cups all-purpose flour
¾ teaspoon baking soda
½ cup finely chopped pecans
Chocolate Chip Glaze (recipe follows)

Melt peanut butter chips and butter in medium saucepan over low heat, stirring constantly. Pour into large mixer bowl; add brown sugar, egg and vanilla, beating until well blended. Stir in flour, baking soda and pecans; blend well. Cover and chill 15 to 20 minutes or until firm enough to roll.

Preheat oven to 350°F. Roll out dough, a small portion at a time, to ¼-inch thickness on lightly floured surface. (Keep remaining dough in refrigerator.) With cookie cutters, cut into desired shapes. Place 2 inches apart on ungreased cookie sheets.

Bake 7 to 8 minutes or until almost set (do not overbake). Cool 1 minute. Remove to wire racks to cool completely. Drizzle Chocolate Chip Glaze onto each cookie; allow to set.

Makes about 3 dozen cookies

Chocolate Chip Glaze: Melt 1 cup HERSHEY'S Semi-Sweet Chocolate Chips with 1 tablespoon shortening in top of double boiler over hot, not boiling, water; stir until smooth. Remove from heat; cool slightly, stirring occasionally.

Peanut Butter Cutout Cookies

Cream Cheese Cutout Cookies

CREAM CHEESE CUTOUT COOKIES

1 cup butter, softened
1 package (8 ounces) cream cheese, softened
1½ cups sugar
1 egg
1 teaspoon vanilla

½ teaspoon almond extract
3½ cups all-purpose flour
1 teaspoon baking powder
Almond Frosting (recipe follows)
Assorted candies for decoration (optional)

In large bowl, beat butter and cream cheese until well combined. Add sugar; beat until fluffy. Add egg, vanilla and almond extract; beat well. In small bowl, combine flour and baking powder. Add dry ingredients to cream cheese mixture; beat until well mixed. Divide dough in half. Wrap each portion in plastic wrap; refrigerate about 1½ hours.

Preheat oven to 375°F. Roll out dough, half at a time, to ⅛-inch thickness on lightly floured surface. Cut out with cookie cutters. Place 2 inches apart on ungreased cookie sheets.

Bake 8 to 10 minutes or until edges are lightly browned. Remove to wire racks to cool completely. Frost cookies with Almond Frosting; decorate with assorted candies, if desired.

Makes about 7 dozen cookies

Almond Frosting: In small bowl, beat 2 cups sifted powdered sugar, 2 tablespoons softened butter and ¼ teaspoon almond extract until smooth. For piping consistency, beat in 4 to 5 teaspoons milk. For spreading consistency, add a little more milk. If desired, tint with food coloring.

Favorite recipe from Wisconsin Milk Marketing Board

CONFETTI CUTOUTS

COOKIES
1½ cups sugar
⅔ cup butter or margarine, softened
2 eggs
1 tablespoon milk

1½ teaspoons almond extract
3½ cups all-purpose flour
2½ teaspoons baking powder
½ teaspoon salt

FILLING
¼ cup vegetable shortening

1½ cups "M&M's"® Plain Chocolate
    Candies

For cookies, in large bowl beat together sugar and butter until light and fluffy; blend in eggs, milk and extract. In bowl combine flour, baking powder and salt. Gradually add dry ingredients to butter mixture, mixing well after each addition. Cover and chill dough several hours.

Preheat oven to 400°F. Roll out dough, one fourth at a time, to ⅛-inch thickness on floured surface. Cut with floured 2½-inch cookie cutters. Cut out small designs in centers of half the cookies with smaller cutter or sharp knife. Place 2 inches apart on ungreased cookie sheets.

Bake 7 to 9 minutes or until edges are very light golden brown. Remove to wire racks to cool completely.

For filling, melt shortening in 2-quart heavy saucepan; add candies. Cook over very low heat, stirring constantly with metal spoon and pressing candies with back of spoon to break up. (Chocolate will be almost melted and pieces of color coating will remain.) Cool slightly or until of spreading consistency. Spread solid cookies with warm filling; top with cutout cookies, pressing lightly to secure. Chill about 30 minutes to set chocolate. Store at room temperature. *Makes about 3 dozen cookies*

LEMON CUTOUT COOKIES

2¾ cups unsifted all-purpose flour
1 teaspoon baking powder
½ teaspoon baking soda
¼ teaspoon salt
1½ cups sugar
½ cup margarine or butter, softened

1 egg
⅓ cup REALEMON® Lemon Juice from
    Concentrate
Lemon Icing (page 35) (optional)

Sift together flour, baking powder, baking soda and salt; set aside. In large mixer bowl, beat sugar and margarine until fluffy; beat in egg. Gradually add dry ingredients alternately with ReaLemon® brand; mix well (dough will be soft). Cover and chill overnight in refrigerator or 2 hours in freezer.

Preheat oven to 375°F. Grease cookie sheets. On well-floured surface, roll out dough, one third at a time, to ⅛-inch thickness; cut with floured cookie cutters. Place 1 inch apart on prepared cookie sheets.

Bake 8 to 10 minutes. Remove to wire racks to cool completely. Repeat with remaining dough. Ice and decorate as desired.   *Makes 4 to 5 dozen cookies*

Lemon Icing: Mix 1¼ cups confectioners' sugar and 2 tablespoons ReaLemon® brand until smooth. Add food coloring, if desired.   *Makes about ½ cup*

Lemon Cutout Cookies

COCOA GINGERBREAD COOKIES

¼ cup butter or margarine, softened
2 tablespoons shortening
⅓ cup packed brown sugar
¼ cup dark molasses
1 egg
1½ cups all-purpose flour
¼ cup unsweetened cocoa

½ teaspoon baking soda
½ teaspoon ground ginger
½ teaspoon ground cinnamon
¼ teaspoon salt
¼ teaspoon ground nutmeg
⅛ teaspoon ground cloves
Decorator Icing (recipe follows)

Preheat oven to 400°F. Lightly grease cookie sheets or line with parchment paper. Beat butter, shortening, brown sugar and molasses in large bowl. Add egg; beat until light. Combine flour, cocoa, baking soda, ginger, cinnamon, salt, nutmeg and cloves in small bowl. Blend into creamed mixture until smooth. (If dough is too soft to handle, cover and refrigerate until firm.)

Roll out dough to ¼-inch thickness on lightly floured surface. Cut out with cookie cutters. Place 2 inches apart on prepared cookie sheets. Bake 8 to 10 minutes or until firm. Remove to wire racks to cool completely. Prepare Decorator Icing. Spoon into pastry bag fitted with small tip. Decorate cookies with icing.

Makes about 6 dozen cookies

Decorator Icing: Beat 1 egg white* in large bowl until frothy. Gradually beat in 3½ cups powdered sugar until blended. Add 1 teaspoon almond or lemon extract and enough water (2 to 3 tablespoons) to moisten. Beat until smooth and glossy.

*Use clean, uncracked egg.

PEANUT BUTTER GINGERBREAD MEN

5 cups all-purpose flour
1½ teaspoons ground cinnamon
1 teaspoon baking soda
½ teaspoon ground ginger
¼ teaspoon salt
¾ cup MAZOLA® Margarine, softened

¾ cup SKIPPY® Creamy Peanut Butter
1 cup packed brown sugar
1 cup KARO® Dark Corn Syrup
2 eggs
Frosting for decorating (optional)

In large bowl, combine flour, cinnamon, baking soda, ginger and salt. In another large bowl, beat margarine and peanut butter until well blended. Add brown sugar, corn syrup and eggs; beat until smooth. Gradually beat in 2 cups of the dry ingredients. With wooden spoon, beat in remaining dry ingredients, 1 cup at a time, until well blended. Divide dough into thirds. Wrap in plastic wrap; chill until firm, at least 1 hour.

Preheat oven to 300°F. Roll out dough, one third at a time, to ⅛-inch thickness on lightly floured surface. Cut out with 5½-inch gingerbread cutter. Place 2 inches apart on ungreased cookie sheets. Bake 10 to 12 minutes or until lightly browned. Remove to wire racks to cool completely. Pipe frosting on cookies to make eyes and buttons, if desired.

Makes about 2½ dozen cookies

CHOCOLATE KAHLÚA® BEARS

¼ cup KAHLÚA®
2 squares (1 ounce each)
    unsweetened chocolate
1⅔ cups sugar
⅔ cup shortening
2 eggs

2 teaspoons vanilla
2 cups sifted all-purpose flour
2 teaspoons baking powder
¾ teaspoon salt
½ teaspoon ground cinnamon
Chocolate Icing (recipe follows)

To Kahlúa® in measuring cup, add enough water to make ⅓ cup liquid. In small saucepan over low heat, melt chocolate; cool. In large bowl, beat sugar, shortening, eggs and vanilla until light and fluffy. Stir in chocolate. In small bowl, combine flour, baking powder, salt and cinnamon. Add dry ingredients to egg mixture alternately with ⅓ cup liquid. Cover; chill until firm.

Preheat oven to 350°F. Roll out dough, one fourth at a time, to ¼-inch thickness on well-floured surface. Cut out with bear-shaped cookie cutters. Place 2 inches apart on ungreased cookie sheets.

Bake 8 to 10 minutes. Remove to wire racks to cool completely. Prepare Chocolate Icing. Spread icing in thin, even layer on cookies. Let stand until set; decorate as desired.   *Makes about 2½ dozen cookies*

Chocolate Icing: In medium saucepan, combine 6 squares (1 ounce each) semisweet chocolate, ⅓ cup butter or margarine, ¼ cup Kahlúa® and 1 tablespoon light corn syrup. Cook over low heat until chocolate melts, stirring to blend. Add ¾ cup sifted powdered sugar; beat until smooth. If necessary, beat in additional Kahlúa® to make spreading consistency.

DUTCH ST. NICHOLAS COOKIES

¾ cup butter or margarine, softened
½ cup packed brown sugar
2 tablespoons milk
1½ teaspoons ground cinnamon
¼ teaspoon ground nutmeg
¼ teaspoon ground ginger

¼ teaspoon ground cloves
2 cups sifted all-purpose flour
1½ teaspoons baking powder
½ teaspoon salt
½ cup toasted chopped almonds
¼ cup coarsely chopped citron

In large bowl, cream butter, sugar, milk and spices. In small bowl, combine flour, baking powder and salt. Add flour mixture to creamed mixture; blend well. Stir in almonds and citron. Knead dough slightly to make a ball. Cover; chill until firm.

Preheat oven to 375°F. Grease cookie sheets. Roll out dough to ¼-inch thickness on lightly floured surface. Cut out with cookie cutters. Place 2 inches apart on prepared cookie sheets. Bake 7 to 10 minutes or until lightly browned. Remove to wire racks to cool.   *Makes about 3½ dozen cookies*

Favorite recipe from Almond Board of California

CUTOUT SUGAR COOKIES

1¼ cups granulated sugar
1 cup BUTTER FLAVOR* CRISCO®
   All-Vegetable Shortening
2 eggs
¼ cup light corn syrup or regular
   pancake syrup

1 tablespoon vanilla
3 cups plus 4 tablespoons all-purpose
   flour, divided
¾ teaspoon baking powder
½ teaspoon baking soda
½ teaspoon salt

1. Combine sugar and shortening in large bowl. Beat at medium speed of electric mixer until well blended. Add eggs, corn syrup and vanilla. Beat until light and fluffy.

2. Combine 3 cups flour, baking powder, baking soda and salt in small bowl. Gradually add dry ingredients to shortening mixture at low speed. Mix until well blended.

3. Divide dough into 4 quarters. Cover and refrigerate at least two hours or overnight.

4. Heat oven to 375°F. Spread 1 tablespoon flour on large sheet of waxed paper. Place one quarter of dough on floured paper. Flatten slightly with hands. Turn dough over. Cover with another large sheet of waxed paper. Roll dough to ¼-inch thickness. Remove top layer of waxed paper. Cut out with cookie cutters. Place 2 inches apart on ungreased baking sheet. Roll and cut out remaining dough.

5. Bake at 375°F for 5 to 9 minutes, depending on size of cookies. (Bake smaller, thinner cookies about 5 minutes; larger cookies about 9 minutes.) Cool 2 minutes on baking sheet. Remove to wire racks to cool completely.

Makes 3 to 4 dozen cookies

Hint: Floured pastry cloth and rolling pin cover make rolling out dough easier.

Variations:
Creamy Vanilla Frosting: Combine ½ cup BUTTER FLAVOR* CRISCO® All-Vegetable Shortening, 1 pound (4 cups) confectioners' sugar, ⅓ cup milk and 1 teaspoon vanilla in medium bowl. Beat at low speed of electric mixer until well blended. Scrape bowl. Beat at high speed for 2 minutes or until smooth and creamy. One or 2 drops food color can be used to tint each cup of frosting, if desired. Frost cooled cookies. This frosting works well in decorating tube.

Chocolate-Dipped Sugar Cookies: Combine 1 cup semisweet chocolate chips and 1 teaspoon BUTTER FLAVOR* CRISCO® All-Vegetable Shortening in microwave-safe measuring cup. Microwave at MEDIUM (50% power). Stir after 1 minute. Repeat until smooth. (Or, melt on range top in small saucepan on very low heat.) Dip one end of cooled cookie halfway in chocolate. Place on waxed paper until chocolate is firm.

Chocolate Nut Sugar Cookies: Dip cooled cookie in melted chocolate as directed for Chocolate-Dipped Sugar Cookies. Spread with finely chopped nuts before chocolate hardens.

*BUTTER FLAVOR CRISCO® is artificially flavored.

Cutout Sugar Cookies

Heavenly Chocolate

Chocolate lovers, look no further! All the cookies in this chapter are chocolatey-good—some are even drizzled with or dipped into luscious chocolate!

CHOCOLATE CHERRY COOKIES

2 squares (1 ounce each) unsweetened chocolate
½ cup butter or margarine, softened
½ cup sugar
1 egg
2 cups cake flour

1 teaspoon vanilla
¼ teaspoon salt
Maraschino cherries, well drained (about 48)
1 cup (6 ounces) semisweet or milk chocolate chips

Melt unsweetened chocolate in top of double boiler over hot, not boiling, water. Remove from heat; cool. Beat butter and sugar in large bowl until light and fluffy. Add egg and melted chocolate; beat until light and fluffy. Stir in flour, vanilla and salt; mix until well blended. Cover; refrigerate until firm, about 1 hour.

Preheat oven to 400°F. Lightly grease cookie sheets or line with parchment paper. Shape dough into 1-inch balls. Place 2 inches apart on prepared cookie sheets. With knuckle of finger, make deep indentation in center of each ball. Place a cherry into each indentation.

Bake 8 minutes or just until set. Meanwhile, melt chocolate chips in small bowl over hot water. Stir until melted. Remove cookies to wire racks to cool. Drizzle melted chocolate over tops while still warm. Refrigerate until chocolate is set.

Makes about 4 dozen cookies

Top to bottom: Chocolate Spritz (page 43); Chocolate Cherry Cookies; Triple Chocolate Pretzels (page 42)

TRIPLE CHOCOLATE PRETZELS

Buttery pretzel-shaped chocolate cookies are glazed with dark chocolate, then decorated with white chocolate for a triple chocolate treat.

2 squares (1 ounce each) unsweetened chocolate	2 cups cake flour
½ cup butter or margarine, softened	1 teaspoon vanilla
½ cup granulated sugar	¼ teaspoon salt
1 egg	Mocha Glaze (recipe follows)
	2 ounces white chocolate, chopped

Melt unsweetened chocolate in top of double boiler over hot, not boiling, water. Remove from heat; cool. Beat butter and granulated sugar in large bowl until light and fluffy. Add egg and melted chocolate; beat until fluffy. Stir in cake flour, vanilla and salt until well blended. Cover; chill until firm, about 1 hour.

Preheat oven to 400°F. Lightly grease cookie sheets or line with parchment paper. Divide dough into 4 equal parts. Divide each part into 12 pieces. To form pretzels, knead each piece briefly to soften dough. Roll into a rope about 6 inches long. Form each rope on prepared cookie sheets into pretzel shape. Repeat with all pieces of dough, spacing cookies 2 inches apart.

Bake 7 to 9 minutes or until firm. Remove to wire racks to cool. Prepare Mocha Glaze. Dip pretzels, one at a time, into glaze to coat completely. Place on waxed paper, right side up. Let stand until glaze is set. Melt white chocolate in small bowl over hot water. Squeeze melted chocolate through pastry bag or drizzle over pretzels to decorate. Let stand until chocolate is completely set.   *Makes 4 dozen cookies*

MOCHA GLAZE

1 cup (6 ounces) semisweet chocolate chips	1 cup powdered sugar
1 teaspoon light corn syrup	3 to 5 tablespoons hot coffee or water
1 teaspoon shortening	

Combine chocolate chips, corn syrup and shortening in small heavy saucepan. Stir over low heat until chocolate is melted. Stir in powdered sugar and enough coffee to make a smooth glaze.

CHOCOLATE SPRITZ

2 squares (1 ounce each)
   unsweetened chocolate
1 cup butter, softened
½ cup granulated sugar
1 egg

1 teaspoon vanilla
¼ teaspoon salt
2¼ cups all-purpose flour
   Powdered sugar

Preheat oven to 400°F. Line cookie sheets with parchment paper or leave ungreased. Melt chocolate in top of double boiler over hot, not boiling, water. Remove from heat; cool. Beat butter, granulated sugar, egg, vanilla and salt in large bowl until light and fluffy. Blend in melted chocolate and flour until stiff. Fit cookie press with your choice of plate. Load press with dough. Press cookies out 2 inches apart onto prepared cookie sheets.

Bake 5 to 7 minutes or just until very slightly browned around edges. Remove to wire racks to cool. Dust with powdered sugar.
Makes about 5 dozen cookies

CHOCOLATE COOKIE SANDWICHES

½ cup shortening
1 cup sugar
1 egg
1 teaspoon vanilla extract
1½ cups all-purpose flour

⅓ cup HERSHEY₂'S Cocoa
½ teaspoon baking soda
½ teaspoon salt
¼ cup milk
   Creme Filling (recipe follows)

Preheat oven to 375°F. In large bowl, beat shortening, sugar, egg and vanilla until light and fluffy. Combine flour, cocoa, baking soda and salt; add alternately with milk to sugar mixture until ingredients are combined. Drop by teaspoonfuls onto ungreased cookie sheets.

Bake 11 to 12 minutes or just until soft-set *(do not overbake)*. Cool 1 minute. Remove from cookie sheets; cool completely on wire racks. Prepare Creme Filling. Spread bottom of one cookie with about 1 tablespoon filling; cover with another cookie. Repeat with remaining cookies and filling.
Makes about 2 dozen sandwich cookies

Creme Filling: In small bowl, beat 2 tablespoons softened butter or margarine and 2 tablespoons shortening; gradually beat in ½ cup marshmallow creme. Blend in ¾ teaspoon vanilla extract and ⅔ cup powdered sugar; beat to spreading consistency.

CHOCOLATE MADELEINES

1¼ cups all-purpose flour
1 cup sugar
⅛ teaspoon salt
¾ cup butter, melted
⅓ cup HERSHEY'S Cocoa

3 eggs
2 egg yolks
½ teaspoon vanilla extract
Chocolate Frosting (recipe follows)

Preheat oven to 350°F. Lightly grease indentations of madeleine mold pan (each shell is 3×2 inches). In medium saucepan, stir together flour, sugar and salt. Combine melted butter and cocoa; stir into dry ingredients. In small bowl, lightly beat eggs, egg yolks and vanilla with fork until well blended; stir into chocolate mixture, blending well. Cook over very low heat, stirring constantly, until mixture is warm; *do not simmer or boil.* Remove from heat. Fill each mold half full with batter (do not overfill).

Bake 8 to 10 minutes or until wooden pick inserted in center comes out clean. Invert onto wire rack; cool completely. Prepare Chocolate Frosting; frost flat sides of cookies. Press frosted sides together, forming shells.

Makes about 1½ dozen filled cookies

Chocolate Frosting: In small bowl, stir together 1¼ cups powdered sugar and 2 tablespoons HERSHEY'S Cocoa. In small bowl, beat 2 tablespoons softened butter and ¼ cup of the cocoa mixture until light and fluffy. Gradually add remaining cocoa mixture and 2 to 2½ tablespoons milk, beating to spreading consistency. Stir in ½ teaspoon vanilla extract.

TRIPLE CHOCOLATE COOKIES

1 package DUNCAN HINES® Moist
    Deluxe Swiss Chocolate Cake Mix
½ cup butter or margarine, melted
1 egg
½ cup semisweet chocolate chips

½ cup milk chocolate chips
½ cup coarsely chopped white
    chocolate
½ cup chopped pecans

1. Preheat oven to 375°F. Combine cake mix, melted butter and egg in large bowl. Stir in all 3 chocolates and pecans.

2. Drop by rounded tablespoonfuls 2 inches apart onto ungreased cookie sheets. Bake 9 to 11 minutes. Cool 1 minute on cookie sheets. Remove to wire racks to cool completely.

Makes 3½ to 4 dozen cookies

Chocolate Madeleines

Chocolate Nut Slices

CHOCOLATE NUT SLICES

COOKIES

1½ cups firmly packed light brown
    sugar
⅔ cup CRISCO® All-Vegetable
    Shortening
1 tablespoon water
1 teaspoon vanilla
2 eggs

1½ cups all-purpose flour
⅓ cup unsweetened baking cocoa
½ teaspoon salt
¼ teaspoon baking soda
1 cup (6-ounce package) semisweet
    chocolate chips
¾ cup chopped pecans

DRIZZLE

½ teaspoon BUTTER FLAVOR*
    CRISCO® All-Vegetable
    Shortening

½ cup white melting chocolate, cut
    into small pieces
Chopped pecans (optional)

1. Heat oven to 375°F.

2. **For cookies,** combine brown sugar, ⅔ cup shortening, water and vanilla in large bowl. Beat at medium speed of electric mixer until well blended. Beat eggs into brown sugar mixture. Combine flour, cocoa, salt and baking soda in small bowl. Mix into shortening mixture at low speed just until blended. Stir in chocolate chips and ¾ cup pecans.

3. Divide dough into 4 equal portions. Form each portion into 8-inch rolls on waxed paper. Pick up ends of waxed paper and roll dough back and forth to get a nicely shaped roll. Place 3 inches apart on ungreased baking sheets.

4. Bake at 375°F for 8 to 10 minutes or until set. Cool on baking sheets.

5. **For drizzle,** combine ½ teaspoon shortening and white chocolate in microwave-safe cup. Microwave at MEDIUM (50% power). Stir after 1 minute. Repeat until smooth. (Or, melt on range top in small saucepan on low heat.) Drizzle back and forth over cooled cookies. Sprinkle with pecans before chocolate hardens, if desired. Cut diagonally into 1-inch slices.   *Makes about 3 dozen cookies*

*BUTTER FLAVOR CRISCO® is artificially flavored.

BROWNIE COOKIE BITES

1½ cups (from 10-ounce package) NESTLÉ® Toll House® Semi-Sweet Chocolate Morsels, divided	**¼ teaspoon baking powder**
1 tablespoon butter	**1 egg**
¼ cup all-purpose flour	**⅓ cup sugar**
	½ teaspoon vanilla extract

Over hot, not boiling, water, melt ½ cup morsels and butter, stirring until smooth.* In small bowl, combine flour and baking powder; set aside.

Preheat oven to 350°F. Grease cookie sheets. In small mixer bowl, beat egg and sugar at high speed until mixture is thick, about 3 minutes. Stir in vanilla and melted chocolate mixture. Gradually blend in flour mixture; stir in remaining 1 cup morsels. Drop by level measuring tablespoonfuls onto prepared cookie sheets.

Bake 8 to 10 minutes or until cookies are puffed and tops are cracked and moist. (Cookies will look slightly underbaked.) Let stand on cookie sheets 5 minutes; cool.   *Makes about 1½ dozen cookies*

*Or, place morsels and butter in microwave-safe bowl. Microwave on HIGH (100% power) 1 minute; stir. Microwave on HIGH (100% power) 30 seconds longer; stir until smooth.

Bevy of Bars

*Easy-to-make bars are always a favorite. Choose
from buttery shortbreads, fruit-topped bars,
spice bars and fudgy brownies.*

PECAN DATE BARS

CRUST
⅓ cup cold butter or margarine
1 package DUNCAN HINES® Moist
   Deluxe White Cake Mix

1 egg

TOPPING
1 package (8 ounces) chopped dates
1¼ cups chopped pecans
1 cup water

½ teaspoon vanilla extract
Confectioners' sugar

1. Preheat oven to 350°F. Grease and flour 13×9-inch baking pan.

2. For crust, cut butter into cake mix with pastry blender or 2 knives until mixture is crumbly. Add egg; stir well (mixture will be crumbly). Pat mixture into bottom of pan.

3. For topping, combine dates, pecans and water in medium saucepan. Bring to a boil. Reduce heat and simmer until mixture thickens, stirring constantly. Remove from heat. Stir in vanilla extract. Spread date mixture evenly over crust. Bake 25 to 30 minutes. Cool completely in pan on wire rack. Dust with confectioners' sugar. *Makes 32 bars*

Tip: Pecan Date Bars are moist and store well in airtight containers. Dust with confectioners' sugar to freshen before serving.

Pecan Date Bars

Almond Toffee Triangles

ALMOND TOFFEE TRIANGLES

Bar Cookie Crust (page 63)
⅓ **cup packed brown sugar**
⅓ **cup KARO® Light or Dark Corn**
   Syrup

¼ **cup MAZOLA® Margarine**
¼ **cup heavy cream**
1½ **cups sliced almonds**
1 **teaspoon vanilla**

Preheat oven to 350°F. Prepare Bar Cookie Crust. In medium saucepan, combine brown sugar, corn syrup, margarine and cream. Bring to a boil over medium heat; remove from heat. Stir in almonds and vanilla. Pour over hot crust; spread evenly.

Bake 15 to 20 minutes or until set and golden. Cool completely on wire rack. Cut into 2½-inch squares; cut each in half diagonally to create triangles.

Makes 4 dozen triangles

DELUXE TOLL HOUSE® MUD BARS

**1 cup plus 2 tablespoons all-purpose
   flour**
½ teaspoon baking soda
½ teaspoon salt
¾ cup firmly packed brown sugar
½ cup (1 stick) butter, softened

1 teaspoon vanilla extract
1 egg
**2 cups (12-ounce package) NESTLÉ®
   Toll House® Semi-Sweet
   Chocolate Morsels, divided**
½ cup chopped walnuts

Preheat oven to 375°F. Grease 9-inch square baking pan. In small bowl, combine flour, baking soda and salt; set aside. In large mixer bowl, beat brown sugar, butter and vanilla extract until creamy. Beat in egg. Gradually add flour mixture. Stir in 1⅓ cups morsels and walnuts. Spread into prepared pan. Bake 23 to 25 minutes.

Immediately sprinkle remaining ⅔ cup morsels over top. Let stand until morsels become shiny and soft. Spread chocolate with spatula. When cool, chill in refrigerator 5 to 10 minutes to set chocolate. Cut into 2×1½-inch bars. *Makes 2 dozen bars*

PECAN CARAMEL BARS

1½ cups all-purpose flour
1½ cups packed brown sugar, divided
½ cup butter, softened

1 cup pecan halves
⅔ cup butter
1 cup milk chocolate pieces

Preheat oven to 350°F. In large mixer bowl, combine flour, 1 cup brown sugar and ½ cup butter. Beat 2 to 3 minutes or until mixture resembles fine crumbs. Pat mixture evenly onto bottom of ungreased 13×9-inch baking pan. Sprinkle nuts evenly over crumb mixture.

In small saucepan, combine ⅔ cup butter and remaining ½ cup brown sugar. Cook and stir over medium heat until entire surface is bubbly. Cook and stir up to 1 minute more. Pour over crust, spreading evenly.

Bake 18 to 20 minutes or until entire surface is bubbly. Remove from oven; immediately sprinkle with chocolate pieces. Let stand 2 to 3 minutes to allow chocolate to melt; use knife to swirl chocolate slightly. Cool completely on wire rack. Cut into bars. *Makes 4 dozen bars*

Favorite recipe from Wisconsin Milk Marketing Board

PEANUT BUTTER BARS

1 package DUNCAN HINES® Peanut
    Butter Cookie Mix
2 egg whites
½ cup chopped peanuts

1 cup confectioners' sugar
2 tablespoons water
½ teaspoon vanilla extract

1. Preheat oven to 350°F.

2. Combine cookie mix, peanut butter packet from Mix and egg whites in large bowl. Stir until thoroughly blended. Press into ungreased 13×9-inch pan. Sprinkle peanuts over dough. Press lightly. Bake 16 to 18 minutes or until golden brown. Cool completely in pan on wire rack. Combine confectioners' sugar, water and vanilla extract in small bowl. Stir until blended. Drizzle glaze over top. Cut into bars.

Makes 24 bars

ENGLISH TOFFEE BARS

2 cups all-purpose flour
1 cup packed light brown sugar
½ cup butter
1 cup pecan halves

Toffee Topping (recipe follows)
1 cup HERSHEY®'S Milk Chocolate
    Chips

Preheat oven to 350°F. In large mixer bowl, combine flour, brown sugar and butter; mix until fine crumbs form. (A few large crumbs may remain.) Press into ungreased 13×9-inch baking pan. Sprinkle pecans over crust. Prepare Toffee Topping and immediately drizzle over pecans and crust.

Bake 20 to 22 minutes or until topping is bubbly and golden. Remove from oven. Immediately sprinkle milk chocolate chips over top; press gently onto surface. Cool completely in pan on wire rack. Cut into bars.

Makes about 3 dozen bars

Toffee Topping: In small saucepan, over medium heat, combine ⅔ cup butter and ⅓ cup packed light brown sugar. Cook, stirring constantly, until mixture comes to a boil. Continue boiling and stirring 30 seconds; use immediately.

Peanut Butter Bars

CHOCOLATE CHERRY BROWNIES

1 jar (16 ounces) maraschino
   cherries
⅔ cup (1 stick plus 3 tablespoons)
   margarine
1 package (6 ounces) semisweet
   chocolate pieces (1 cup), divided
1 cup sugar
1 teaspoon vanilla

2 eggs
1¼ cups all-purpose flour
¾ cup QUAKER® Oats (Quick or Old
   Fashioned), uncooked
1 teaspoon baking powder
¼ teaspoon salt (optional)
½ cup chopped nuts (optional)
2 teaspoons vegetable shortening

Preheat oven to 350°F. Lightly grease 13×9-inch baking pan. Drain cherries; reserve 12 and chop remainder. In large saucepan over low heat, melt margarine and ½ cup chocolate pieces, stirring until smooth. Remove from heat; cool slightly. Add sugar and vanilla. Beat in eggs, one at a time. Add combined flour, oats, baking powder and salt. Stir in chopped cherries and nuts. Spread into prepared pan.

Bake about 25 minutes or until brownies pull away from sides of pan. Cool completely in pan on wire rack.

Cut reserved cherries in half; place evenly on top of brownies. In saucepan over low heat, melt remaining ½ cup chocolate pieces and vegetable shortening, stirring constantly until smooth. Drizzle over brownies; cut into about 2½-inch squares. Store tightly covered. *Makes about 2 dozen bars*

PECAN MINCE BARS

1½ cups plus 3 tablespoons unsifted
   all-purpose flour, divided
⅓ cup confectioners' sugar
¾ cup cold margarine or butter
4 eggs, beaten
1 (9-ounce) package NONE SUCH®
   Condensed Mincemeat, crumbled

1 cup chopped pecans
⅓ cup firmly packed light brown
   sugar
1 teaspoon grated lemon peel
½ teaspoon baking powder
   Pecan halves (optional)

Preheat oven to 350°F. Lightly grease 13×9-inch baking pan. In small mixer bowl, combine *1½ cups* flour, confectioners' sugar and margarine; mix until crumbly. Press onto bottom of prepared pan. Bake 20 minutes.

Meanwhile, in large bowl, combine remaining *3 tablespoons* flour, eggs, mincemeat, chopped pecans, brown sugar, lemon peel and baking powder; beat well. Spread evenly over baked crust. Bake 20 to 25 minutes more or until set. Cool in pan on wire rack. Garnish with pecan halves, if desired. Cut into bars. Store loosely covered at room temperature. *Makes 2 to 3 dozen bars*

ORANGE PUMPKIN BARS

BARS
1½ cups all-purpose flour
1 teaspoon baking powder
1 teaspoon pumpkin pie spice
½ teaspoon baking soda
½ teaspoon salt
1 cup canned solid-packed pumpkin
    (not pumpkin pie filling)
¾ cup granulated sugar

⅔ cup CRISCO® Oil
2 eggs
¼ cup firmly packed light brown
    sugar
2 tablespoons orange juice
½ cup chopped nuts
½ cup raisins

ICING
1½ cups powdered sugar
2 tablespoons orange juice

2 tablespoons butter or margarine,
    softened
½ teaspoon grated orange peel

1. Preheat oven to 350°F. Grease and flour 12×8-inch baking dish.

2. For bars, combine flour, baking powder, pumpkin pie spice, baking soda and salt in medium mixing bowl. Combine pumpkin, granulated sugar, Crisco® Oil, eggs, brown sugar and orange juice in large mixing bowl. Beat at low speed of electric mixer until blended, scraping bowl constantly. Add flour mixture. Beat at medium speed until smooth, scraping bowl frequently. Stir in nuts and raisins. Pour into prepared pan. Bake about 35 minutes or until center springs back when touched lightly. Cool completely.

3. For icing, combine powdered sugar, orange juice, butter and orange peel. Beat at medium speed of electric mixer until smooth. Spread over cooled bars.   *Makes 24 bars*

LINZER BARS

¾ cup butter or margarine, softened
½ cup sugar
1 egg
½ teaspoon grated lemon peel
½ teaspoon ground cinnamon
¼ teaspoon salt

⅛ teaspoon ground cloves
2 cups all-purpose flour
1 cup DIAMOND® Walnuts, finely
    chopped or ground
1 cup raspberry or apricot jam

Preheat oven to 325°F. Grease 9-inch square pan. In large bowl, cream butter, sugar, egg, lemon peel, cinnamon, salt and cloves. Blend in flour and walnuts. Set aside about ¼ of the dough for lattice top. Pat remaining dough into bottom and about ½ inch up sides of pan. Spread with jam. Make pencil-shaped strips of remaining dough, rolling against floured board with palms of hands. Arrange in lattice pattern over top, pressing ends against dough on sides. Bake 45 minutes or until lightly browned. Cool in pan on wire rack. Cut into bars.   *Makes 2 dozen small bars*

Almond Apricot Bars

ALMOND APRICOT BARS

⅔ cup dried apricots
1⅓ cups all-purpose flour, divided
¼ cup granulated sugar
⅓ cup cold butter
1 cup sliced natural almonds, toasted
   and divided
2 eggs

1 cup packed brown sugar
½ teaspoon vanilla extract
¼ teaspoon almond extract
¼ teaspoon grated lemon peel
1 tablespoon lemon juice
½ teaspoon baking powder

Preheat oven to 350°F. Place apricots in small saucepan; cover with water and bring to a boil. Simmer apricots 10 minutes; drain. Chop apricots and set aside. Blend 1 cup flour with granulated sugar. Cut in butter until mixture resembles cornmeal. Stir in ½ cup almonds. Pat into ungreased 9-inch square pan. Bake 20 minutes.

In large bowl, beat eggs and brown sugar until sugar is dissolved. Blend in vanilla and almond extract, lemon peel and lemon juice. Blend remaining ⅓ cup flour with baking powder in small bowl. Fold into egg mixture. Stir in chopped apricots. Pour over base. Sprinkle with remaining ½ cup almonds. Return to oven; bake 25 minutes. Cool in pan on wire rack. Cut into bars.   *Makes 2 dozen bars*

Favorite recipe from Almond Board of California

PUMPKIN PECAN PIE BARS

1 cup firmly packed brown sugar
½ cup margarine or butter, softened
1½ cups unsifted all-purpose flour
1 cup rolled oats
1 teaspoon baking powder
1 teaspoon salt, divided
1 (16-ounce) can pumpkin
 (about 2 cups)

1 (14-ounce) can EAGLE® Brand
 Sweetened Condensed Milk
 (NOT evaporated milk)
2 eggs, beaten
2 teaspoons pumpkin pie spice
1½ teaspoons vanilla extract
1 cup chopped pecans
 Confectioners' sugar (optional)

Preheat oven to 350°F. In large mixer bowl, beat brown sugar and margarine until fluffy; add flour, oats, baking powder and *½ teaspoon* salt. Mix until crumbly. Reserve ½ cup crumb mixture. Press remaining crumb mixture on bottom of ungreased 15×10-inch baking pan. Bake 20 minutes.

Meanwhile, in medium bowl, combine pumpkin, sweetened condensed milk, eggs, pumpkin pie spice, vanilla and remaining *½ teaspoon* salt. Spread over crust. In small bowl, combine reserved crumb mixture with pecans; sprinkle over pumpkin mixture. Bake 30 to 35 minutes or until set. Cool in pan on wire rack. Sprinkle with confectioners' sugar, if desired. Cut into bars. Store covered in refrigerator.
Makes 3 to 4 dozen bars

APPLESAUCE FRUITCAKE BARS

1 (14-ounce) can EAGLE® Brand
    Sweetened Condensed Milk (NOT
    evaporated milk)
2 eggs
¼ cup margarine or butter, melted
2 teaspoons vanilla extract
3 cups biscuit baking mix
1 (15-ounce) jar applesauce

1 cup chopped dates
1 (6-ounce) container green candied
    cherries, chopped
1 (6-ounce) container red candied
    cherries, chopped
1 cup chopped nuts
1 cup raisins
    Confectioners' sugar

Preheat oven to 325°F. Grease well and flour 15×10-inch baking pan. In large mixer bowl, beat sweetened condensed milk, eggs, margarine and vanilla. Stir in remaining ingredients except confectioners' sugar; mix well. Spread evenly into prepared pan.

Bake 35 to 40 minutes or until wooden pick inserted in center comes out clean. Cool in pan on wire rack. Sprinkle with confectioners' sugar. Cut into bars. Store tightly covered at room temperature.

Makes 3 to 4 dozen bars

Applesauce Fruitcake Bars

ALMOND DREAM BARS

18 graham crackers, divided
¾ cup firmly packed brown sugar
½ cup butter or margarine
½ cup *undiluted* CARNATION®
Evaporated Milk

1 cup graham cracker crumbs
1 cup sliced almonds, divided
1 cup flaked coconut
½ cup chopped dried apricots
Almond Icing (recipe follows)

Grease 8-inch square dish. Line bottom of dish with 9 of the graham crackers. In medium saucepan, combine brown sugar, butter and evaporated milk. Cook over medium heat, stirring constantly, until mixture comes to a full boil. Remove from heat. Immediately stir in graham cracker crumbs, *¾ cup* almonds, coconut and apricots. Spread apricot mixture evenly over graham crackers in dish. Top with remaining 9 graham crackers. Press down firmly. Spread with Almond Icing. Sprinkle with remaining ¼ cup almonds. Chill until firm. Cut into bars. *Makes 32 bars*

Almond Icing: In medium bowl, blend 1½ cups sifted powdered sugar with 2 tablespoons softened butter or margarine. Add 2 tablespoons *undiluted* CARNATION® Evaporated Milk and ½ teaspoon almond extract. Beat until smooth.

BANANA-DATE BARS

3 ripe, medium DOLE® Bananas,
peeled
½ cup margarine, softened
1 cup brown sugar, packed
2 eggs
2 cups all-purpose flour
1 teaspoon baking soda

1 teaspoon ground cinnamon
½ teaspoon baking powder
½ teaspoon ground nutmeg
¼ teaspoon salt
1 cup DOLE® Chopped Dates
1 cup chopped walnuts
Powdered sugar

• Preheat oven to 350°F. Grease 13×9-inch pan.

• Purée 1 banana in blender or food processor, making ½ cup purée.

• Dice remaining 2 bananas.

• Beat margarine and brown sugar in large bowl until light and fluffy. Beat in eggs. Beat in puréed banana.

• Combine dry ingredients in small bowl; beat into banana mixture until well blended. Fold in dates, nuts and diced bananas. Turn batter into prepared pan.

• Bake 25 minutes. Cool in pan on wire rack. Sprinkle with powdered sugar. Cut into bars.
Makes 2 dozen bars

BLONDE BRICKLE BROWNIES

1⅓ cups all-purpose flour
½ teaspoon baking powder
¼ teaspoon salt
2 eggs, room temperature
½ cup granulated sugar
½ cup packed brown sugar

⅓ cup butter or margarine, melted
1 teaspoon vanilla
¼ teaspoon almond extract
1 package (6 ounces) BITS 'O BRICKLE®, divided
½ cup chopped pecans (optional)

Preheat oven to 350°F. Grease 8-inch square baking pan. Combine flour, baking powder and salt; set aside. Beat eggs well. Gradually add granulated and brown sugars; beat until thick and creamy. Add melted butter, vanilla and almond extract. Gently stir in flour mixture until moistened. Fold in ⅔ cup of the Bits 'O Brickle® and nuts. Pour into prepared pan.

Bake 30 minutes. Remove from oven and immediately sprinkle remaining Bits 'O Brickle® over top. Cool completely in pan on wire rack before cutting.

Makes 16 generous bars

HERSHEY®'S PREMIUM DOUBLE CHOCOLATE BROWNIES

¾ cup HERSHEY®'S Cocoa
½ teaspoon baking soda
⅔ cup butter or margarine, melted and divided
½ cup boiling water
2 cups sugar
2 eggs, slightly beaten
1⅓ cups all-purpose flour

1 teaspoon vanilla extract
¼ teaspoon salt
2 cups (12-ounce package) HERSHEY®'S Semi-Sweet Chocolate Chips
½ cup coarsely chopped nuts (optional)

Preheat oven to 350°F. Grease 13×9-inch baking pan. In large bowl, stir together cocoa and baking soda; blend in ⅓ cup melted butter. Add boiling water; stir until mixture thickens. Stir in sugar, eggs and remaining ⅓ cup melted butter; stir until smooth. Add flour, vanilla and salt; blend well. Stir in chocolate chips and nuts, if desired. Pour into prepared pan. Bake 35 to 40 minutes or until brownies begin to pull away from sides of pan. Cool completely in pan on wire rack. Cut into squares.

Makes about 3 dozen bars

Blonde Brickle Brownies

Left to right: Chocolate-Drizzled Peanut Bars; Chocolate Pecan Pie Bars

CHOCOLATE–DRIZZLED PEANUT BARS

Bar Cookie Crust (see page 63)
½ cup packed brown sugar
⅓ cup KARO® Light Corn Syrup
¼ cup MAZOLA® Margarine
¼ cup heavy cream

1 teaspoon vanilla
¼ teaspoon lemon juice
1½ cups coarsely chopped roasted peanuts
Chocolate Glaze (recipe follows)

Preheat oven to 350°F. Prepare Bar Cookie Crust. In medium saucepan, combine brown sugar, corn syrup, margarine and cream. Bring to a boil over medium heat; remove from heat. Stir in vanilla and lemon juice, then peanuts. Pour over hot crust; spread evenly.

Bake 15 to 20 minutes or until set. Cool completely on wire rack. Prepare Chocolate Glaze. Drizzle with glaze; cool before cutting.

Makes about 5 dozen bars

Chocolate Glaze: In small heavy saucepan over low heat, combine ⅔ cup semisweet chocolate chips and 1 tablespoon MAZOLA® Margarine; stir until melted and smooth.

CHOCOLATE PECAN PIE BARS

1⅓ cups all-purpose flour
½ cup plus 2 tablespoons packed light
   brown sugar, divided
½ cup butter or margarine
2 eggs
½ cup light corn syrup

¼ cup HERSHEY,'S Cocoa
2 tablespoons butter or margarine,
   melted
1 teaspoon vanilla extract
⅛ teaspoon salt
1 cup coarsely chopped pecans

Preheat oven to 350°F. In medium bowl stir together flour and 2 tablespoons brown sugar. Cut in ½ cup butter until mixture resembles coarse crumbs; press onto bottom and about 1 inch up sides of 9-inch square baking pan.

Bake 10 to 12 minutes or until set. With back of spoon, lightly press crust into corners and against sides of pan.

Meanwhile, in small bowl lightly beat eggs, corn syrup, remaining ½ cup brown sugar, cocoa, melted butter, vanilla and salt. Stir in pecans. Pour mixture over warm crust.

Return to oven. Bake 25 minutes more or until pecan filling is set. Cool completely in pan on wire rack.
Cut into bars.   *Makes 16 bars*

BAR COOKIE CRUST

MAZOLA® No Stick Cooking Spray
2½ cups all-purpose flour
1 cup cold MAZOLA® Margarine, cut
   in pieces

½ cup confectioners' sugar
¼ teaspoon salt

Preheat oven to 350°F. Spray 15×10×1-inch baking pan with cooking spray. In large bowl with mixer at medium speed, beat flour, margarine, sugar and salt until mixture resembles coarse crumbs; press firmly and evenly into prepared pan.

Bake 20 minutes or until golden brown. Top with desired filling. Finish baking according to individual recipe directions.

MINT CHOCOLATE TRUFFLE BARS

BASE
¾ cup (1½ sticks) butter, softened
1½ cups all-purpose flour

½ cup sugar
2 tablespoons NESTLÉ® Cocoa

TOPPING
1½ cups (10-ounce package) NESTLÉ®
    Toll House® Mint Flavored
    Semi-Sweet Chocolate Morsels
½ cup (1 stick) butter
4 eggs

¼ cup sugar
2 tablespoons all-purpose flour
1 teaspoon vanilla extract
    Confectioners' sugar

Base: Preheat oven to 350°F. In small mixer bowl, beat ¾ cup butter, 1½ cups flour, ½ cup sugar and cocoa until soft dough forms; spread dough into ungreased 13×9-inch baking pan. Bake 8 to 9 minutes or until crust is barely set.

Topping: In small saucepan over very low heat, melt morsels and ½ cup butter, stirring constantly; remove from heat.

In small mixer bowl, beat eggs and ¼ cup sugar until light and fluffy, about 3 minutes. At low speed, beat in 2 tablespoons flour, vanilla extract and melted chocolate. Pour over crust.

Bake 18 minutes or *just* until toothpick inserted in center comes out clean. (Topping may puff and crack, but will flatten as it cools.) Cool in pan on wire rack. Sprinkle with confectioners' sugar. Cut into 1½-inch squares.

Makes about 4 dozen bars

CRANBERRY WALNUT BARS

    Bar Cookie Crust (page 63)
4 eggs
1⅓ cups KARO® Light or Dark Corn
    Syrup
1 cup sugar

3 tablespoons MAZOLA® Margarine,
    melted
2 cups coarsely chopped fresh or
    frozen cranberries
1 cup chopped walnuts

Preheat oven to 350°F. Prepare Bar Cookie Crust. In large bowl, beat eggs, corn syrup, sugar and margarine until well blended. Stir in cranberries and walnuts. Pour over hot crust; spread evenly. Bake 25 to 30 minutes or until set. Cool completely on wire rack before cutting.

Makes 4 dozen bars

CHOCOLATE PEANUT BUTTER SQUARES

1½ cups chocolate-covered graham
    cracker crumbs (about 17
    crackers)
3 tablespoons PARKAY® Margarine,
    melted
1 (8-ounce) package PHILADELPHIA
    BRAND® Cream Cheese, softened

½ cup chunky-style peanut butter
1 cup powdered sugar
¼ cup BAKER'S® Semi-Sweet Real
    Chocolate Chips
1 teaspoon shortening

Preheat oven to 350°F.

Stir together crumbs and margarine in small bowl. Press onto bottom of 9-inch square baking pan. Bake 10 minutes. Cool.

Beat cream cheese, peanut butter and sugar in small mixing bowl at medium speed with electric mixer until well blended. Spread over crust.

Melt chocolate chips with shortening in small saucepan over low heat, stirring until smooth. Drizzle over cream cheese mixture. Chill 6 hours or overnight. Cut into squares.   *Makes about 1 dozen bars*

Microwave Tip: Microwave chocolate chips and shortening in small microwave-safe bowl on HIGH (100% power) 1 to 2 minutes or until chocolate begins to melt, stirring every minute. Stir until chocolate is melted.

Chocolate Peanut Butter Squares

Fancy Cookies

These eye-catching cookies are as delectable as they look! The sensational results are worth the extra time it takes to make them.

BRANDY LACE COOKIES

Reserve these crisp, intriguing cookies for a special occasion. If time is limited, curling the cookies is optional.

¼ cup sugar
¼ cup MAZOLA® Margarine
¼ cup KARO® Light or Dark Corn
    Syrup
½ cup all-purpose flour

¼ cup very finely chopped pecans or
    walnuts
2 tablespoons brandy
    Melted white and/or semisweet
    chocolate (optional)

Preheat oven to 350°F. Lightly grease and flour cookie sheets. In small saucepan combine sugar, margarine and corn syrup. Bring to a boil over medium heat, stirring constantly. Remove from heat. Stir in flour, pecans and brandy. Drop 12 evenly spaced half teaspoonfuls of batter onto prepared cookie sheets.

Bake 6 minutes or until golden. Cool 1 to 2 minutes or until cookies can be lifted but are still warm and pliable; remove with spatula. Curl around handle of wooden spoon; slide off when crisp. If cookies harden before curling, return to oven to soften. Drizzle with melted chocolate, if desired.

Makes 4 to 5 dozen cookies

Top to bottom: Brandy Lace Cookies; Kentucky Bourbon Pecan Tarts (page 73)

Top to bottom: Honey-Ginger Bourbon Balls (page 12);
Chocolate-Frosted Lebkuchen

CHOCOLATE–FROSTED LEBKUCHEN

Lebkuchen are holiday favorites in Germany.

4 eggs
1 cup sugar
1½ cups all-purpose flour
1 cup (6 ounces) pulverized almonds*
⅓ cup candied lemon peel, finely
    chopped
⅓ cup candied orange peel, finely
    chopped

1½ teaspoons ground cinnamon
1 teaspoon grated lemon peel
½ teaspoon ground cardamom
½ teaspoon ground nutmeg
¼ teaspoon ground cloves
    Bittersweet Glaze (recipe follows)

In large bowl of electric mixer, combine eggs and sugar. Beat at high speed for 10 minutes. Meanwhile, in separate bowl, combine flour, almonds, candied lemon and orange peels, cinnamon, grated lemon peel, cardamom, nutmeg and cloves. Blend in egg mixture, stirring until evenly mixed. Cover; refrigerate 12 hours or overnight.

Preheat oven to 350°F. Grease cookie sheets and dust with flour or line with parchment paper. Drop dough by rounded teaspoonfuls 2 inches apart onto prepared cookie sheets.

Bake 8 to 10 minutes or until just barely browned. Do not overbake. Remove to wire racks. While cookies bake, prepare Bittersweet Glaze. Spread over tops of warm cookies using pastry brush. Cool until glaze is set. Store in airtight container.   *Makes about 5 dozen cookies*

*To pulverize almonds, place in food processor or blender. Process until thoroughly ground with a dry, not pasty, texture.

Bittersweet Glaze: Melt 3 chopped squares (1 ounce each) bittersweet or semisweet chocolate and 1 tablespoon butter or margarine in small bowl over hot water. Stir until smooth.

WHITE BROWNIE BITES

4 bars (2 ounces each) NESTLÉ®
 Semi-Sweet Chocolate Baking
 Bars, broken up
2 tablespoons butter or margarine
½ cup all-purpose flour
½ teaspoon baking powder

2 eggs
⅔ cup sugar
1 teaspoon vanilla extract
6 bars (2 ounces each) NESTLÉ®
 Premier White® Baking Bars,
 coarsely chopped

Preheat oven to 350°F. Over hot, not boiling, water, melt chocolate baking bars and butter, stirring until smooth. In small bowl, combine flour and baking powder; set aside.

In small mixer bowl, beat eggs and sugar at high speed until mixture is thick, about 5 minutes. Stir in vanilla extract and melted chocolate mixture. Gradually blend in flour mixture. Stir in white baking bars. Drop by level measuring tablespoonfuls onto greased cookie sheets.

Bake 8 to 10 minutes until cookies are puffed and tops are cracked and moist. (Cookies will look slightly underbaked.) Let stand on cookie sheets 5 minutes; cool.   *Makes about 3 dozen cookies*

ALMOND RICE MADELEINES

Vegetable oil cooking spray
1 cup whole blanched almonds,
    lightly toasted
1½ cups granulated sugar
¾ cup flaked coconut
3 cups cooked rice, chilled

3 egg whites
Fresh raspberries (optional)
Frozen nondairy whipped topping,
    thawed (optional)
Powdered sugar (optional)

Preheat oven to 350°F. Coat madeleine pans* with vegetable oil cooking spray. Place almonds in food processor fitted with knife blade; process until finely ground. Add granulated sugar and coconut to processor; process until coconut is finely minced. Add rice; pulse to blend. Add egg whites; pulse to blend. Spoon mixture evenly into madeleine pans, filling to tops.

Bake 25 to 30 minutes or until lightly browned. Cool completely in pans on wire racks. Cover and refrigerate 2 hours or until serving time. Run a sharp knife around each madeleine shell and gently remove from pan. Invert onto serving plates; serve with raspberries and whipped topping, if desired. Sprinkle with powdered sugar, if desired.   *Makes about 3 dozen madeleines*

*You may substitute miniature muffin pans for madeleine pans.

Favorite recipe from USA Rice Council

MINI MORSEL MERINGUE WREATHS

2 egg whites
¼ teaspoon cream of tartar
⅓ cup sugar
½ cup (from 12-ounce package)
    NESTLÉ® Toll House® Semi-Sweet
    Chocolate Mini Morsels

1 (3-ounce) package candied
    cherries, quartered

Preheat oven to 275°F. In small mixer bowl, beat egg whites and cream of tartar until soft peaks form. Gradually add sugar; beat until stiff peaks form. Fold in morsels. Spoon into pastry bag fitted with plain #7 pastry tip. Pipe 2-inch circles onto parchment paper-lined cookie sheets. Top each wreath with two candied cherry pieces. Bake 20 minutes. Turn oven off; let stand in oven 30 minutes with door ajar. Cool; peel off paper. Store in airtight container.   *Makes 2½ dozen cookies*

Almond Rice Madeleines

CHOCOLATE PISTACHIO FINGERS

Both ends of these buttery, finger-shaped cookies are dipped into melted chocolate. Then, for an elegant finish, the chocolate ends are covered with chopped pistachios.

¾ cup butter or margarine, softened
⅓ cup sugar
3 ounces (about ⅓ cup) almond paste
1 egg yolk
1⅔ cups all-purpose flour

1 cup (6 ounces) semisweet chocolate chips
½ cup finely chopped natural pistachios

Preheat oven to 350°F. Line cookie sheets with parchment paper or lightly grease and dust with flour. Beat butter and sugar in large bowl until blended. Add almond paste and egg yolk; beat until light. Blend in flour to make a smooth dough. (If dough is too soft to handle, cover and refrigerate until firm.)

Turn out onto lightly floured board. Divide into 8 equal pieces; divide each piece in half. Roll each half into a 12-inch rope; cut each rope into 2-inch lengths. Place 2 inches apart on prepared cookie sheets.

Bake 10 to 12 minutes or until edges just begin to brown. Remove to wire racks to cool.

Melt chocolate chips in small bowl over hot water. Stir until smooth. Dip both ends of cookies about ½ inch into melted chocolate, then dip the chocolate ends into pistachios. Place on waxed paper; let stand until chocolate is set. *Makes about 8 dozen cookies*

Chocolate Pistachio Fingers; Chocolate-Dipped Oat Cookies (page 79)

KENTUCKY BOURBON PECAN TARTS

These bite-size Southern favorites are ideal for a dessert buffet. For added convenience, prepare ahead and keep frozen for up to two weeks.

Cream Cheese Pastry (recipe follows)
2 eggs
½ cup granulated sugar
½ cup KARO® Light or Dark Corn Syrup

2 tablespoons bourbon
1 tablespoon MAZOLA® Margarine, melted
½ teaspoon vanilla
1 cup chopped pecans
Confectioners' sugar (optional)

Preheat oven to 350°F. Prepare Cream Cheese Pastry. Divide dough in half; set aside one half. On floured surface roll out pastry to ⅛-inch thickness. *If necessary, add small amount of flour to keep pastry from sticking.* Cut into 12 (2¼-inch) rounds. Press evenly into bottoms and up sides of 1¾-inch muffin pan cups. Repeat with remaining pastry. Refrigerate.

In medium bowl, beat eggs slightly. Stir in granulated sugar, corn syrup, bourbon, margarine and vanilla until well blended. Spoon 1 heaping teaspoon pecans into each pastry-lined cup; top with 1 tablespoon corn syrup mixture.

Bake 20 to 25 minutes or until lightly browned and toothpick inserted into center comes out clean. Cool in pans 5 minutes. Remove; cool completely on wire rack. If desired, sprinkle with confectioners' sugar.

Makes about 2 dozen tarts

CREAM CHEESE PASTRY

1 cup all-purpose flour
¾ teaspoon baking powder
Pinch salt
½ cup MAZOLA® Margarine, softened

1 package (3 ounces) cream cheese, softened
2 teaspoons sugar

In small bowl combine flour, baking powder and salt. In large bowl mix margarine, cream cheese and sugar until well combined. Stir in flour mixture until well blended. Press firmly into ball with hands.

DOUBLE–DIPPED HAZELNUT CRISPS

¾ cup semisweet chocolate chips
1¼ cups all-purpose flour
¾ cup powdered sugar
⅔ cup whole hazelnuts, toasted,
    hulled and pulverized*
¼ teaspoon instant espresso coffee
    powder

Dash salt
½ cup butter or margarine, softened
2 teaspoons vanilla
4 squares (1 ounce each) bittersweet
    or semisweet chocolate
4 ounces white chocolate
2 teaspoons shortening, divided

Preheat oven to 350°F. Lightly grease cookie sheets or line with parchment paper. Melt chocolate chips in top of double boiler over hot, not boiling, water. Remove from heat; cool. Blend flour, sugar, hazelnuts, coffee powder and salt in large bowl. Blend in butter, melted chocolate and vanilla until dough is stiff but smooth. (If dough is too soft to handle, cover and refrigerate until firm.)

Roll out dough, one fourth at a time, to ⅛-inch thickness on lightly floured surface. Cut out with 2-inch scalloped round cutter. Place 2 inches apart on prepared cookie sheets.

Bake 8 minutes or until not quite firm. (Cookies should not brown. They will puff up during baking and then fall again.) Remove to wire racks to cool.

Place bittersweet and white chocolates in separate small bowls. Add 1 teaspoon shortening to each bowl. Place bowls over hot water; stir until chocolates are melted and smooth. Dip cookies, one at a time, halfway into bittersweet chocolate. Place on waxed paper; refrigerate until chocolate is set. Dip other halves of cookies into white chocolate; refrigerate until set. Store cookies in airtight container in cool place. (If cookies are frozen, chocolate may discolor.)   *Makes about 4 dozen cookies*

*To pulverize hazelnuts, place in food processor or blender. Process until thoroughly ground with a dry, not pasty, texture.

Double-Dipped Hazelnut Crisps; Pecan Florentines (page 76)

PECAN FLORENTINES

Florentines are lacy confections that require a bit more skill to prepare than the average drop cookie. When baked on foil as directed, they are much easier to handle.

¾ **cup pecan halves, pulverized***   ¼ **cup butter or margarine**
½ **cup all-purpose flour**   2 **tablespoons milk**
⅓ **cup packed brown sugar**   ⅓ **cup semisweet chocolate chips**
¼ **cup light corn syrup**

Preheat oven to 350°F. Line cookie sheets with foil; lightly grease foil. Combine pecans and flour in small bowl. Combine brown sugar, corn syrup, butter and milk in medium saucepan. Stir over medium heat until mixture comes to a boil. Remove from heat; stir in flour mixture. Drop batter by teaspoonfuls about 3 inches apart onto prepared cookie sheets.

Bake 10 to 12 minutes or until lacy and golden brown. (Cookies are soft when hot, but become crisp as they cool.) Remove cookies by lifting foil from cookie sheet; set foil on flat, heat-proof surface. Cool cookies completely on foil.

Place chocolate chips in small heavy-duty plastic bag; close securely. Set bag in bowl of hot water until chips are melted, being careful not to let any water into bag. (Knead bag lightly to check that chips are completely melted.) Pat bag dry. With scissors, snip off a small corner from one side of bag. Squeeze melted chocolate over cookies to decorate. Let stand until chocolate is set. Peel cookies off foil.

Makes about 3 dozen cookies

*To pulverize pecans, place in food processor or blender. Process until thoroughly ground with a dry, not pasty, texture.

PINWHEEL COOKIES

1¼ **cups granulated sugar**   1 **tablespoon vanilla**
1 **cup BUTTER FLAVOR* CRISCO®**   3 **cups all-purpose flour**
    All-Vegetable Shortening   ¾ **teaspoon baking powder**
2 **eggs**   ½ **teaspoon baking soda**
¼ **cup light corn syrup or regular**   ½ **teaspoon salt**
    pancake syrup   ⅓ **cup cocoa powder**

1. Combine sugar and shortening in large bowl. Beat at medium speed of electric mixer until well blended. Add eggs, corn syrup and vanilla. Beat until light and fluffy.

2. Combine flour, baking powder, baking soda and salt in small bowl. Add gradually to shortening mixture at low speed. Mix until well blended. Divide dough in half.

3. Add cocoa to half of dough. Blend well. Wrap both doughs with plastic wrap. Refrigerate several hours or overnight.

4. Spread 1 tablespoon or more of flour on large sheet of waxed paper. Place chocolate dough on floured paper. Flatten slightly with hands. Turn dough over and cover with another large sheet of waxed paper. Roll dough into 14×9-inch rectangle. Set aside. Repeat procedure with plain dough. Lay plain dough directly on top of chocolate dough. Remove remaining waxed paper. Roll up jelly-roll fashion, beginning at wide side. Cover and refrigerate 2 hours.

5. Heat oven to 375°F. Cut dough into ⅜-inch-thick slices. Place slices 2 inches apart on ungreased baking sheets. Bake at 375°F for 8 to 10 minutes or until cookies are just beginning to brown. Cool 2 minutes on baking sheets. Remove to wire racks to cool completely.

Makes about 3½ to 4 dozen cookies

*BUTTER FLAVOR CRISCO® is artificially flavored.

FANCY WALNUT BROWNIES

BROWNIES
1 package DUNCAN HINES®
    Chocolate Lovers' Walnut
    Brownie Mix
1 egg

⅓ cup water
⅓ cup CRISCO® Oil or CRISCO®
    PURITAN® Oil

GLAZE
4½ cups confectioners' sugar
½ cup milk or water

24 walnut halves, for garnish

CHOCOLATE DRIZZLE
⅓ cup semisweet chocolate chips

1 tablespoon CRISCO® Shortening

1. Preheat oven to 350°F. Place 24 (2-inch) foil liners on baking sheets.

2. **For brownies,** combine brownie mix, egg, water and oil in large bowl. Stir with spoon until well blended, about 50 strokes. Stir in contents of walnut packet from Mix. Fill each foil liner with 2 generous tablespoons batter. Bake at 350°F for 20 to 25 minutes or until set. Cool completely. Remove liners. Turn brownies upside down on cooling racks.

3. **For glaze,** combine confectioners' sugar and milk in medium bowl. Blend until smooth. Spoon glaze over first brownie to completely cover. Top immediately with walnut half. Repeat with remaining brownies. Allow glaze to set.

4. **For chocolate drizzle,** place chocolate chips and shortening in small resealable plastic food storage bag; seal. Place bag in bowl of hot water for several minutes. Dry with paper towel. Knead until blended and chocolate is smooth. Cut pinpoint hole in corner of bag. Drizzle chocolate over brownies. Allow chocolate drizzle to set before storing in single layer in airtight container.

Makes 24 brownies

Choco-Caramel Delights

CHOCO–CARAMEL DELIGHTS

⅔ cup sugar
½ cup butter or margarine, softened
1 egg, separated
2 tablespoons milk
1 teaspoon vanilla extract
1 cup all-purpose flour
⅓ cup HERSHEY'S Cocoa

¼ teaspoon salt
1 cup finely chopped pecans
Caramel Filling (recipe follows)
½ cup HERSHEY'S Semi-Sweet
Chocolate Chips or Premium
Semi-Sweet Chocolate Chunks
1 teaspoon shortening

In large mixer bowl, beat sugar, butter, egg yolk, milk and vanilla until blended. Stir together flour, cocoa and salt in small bowl; blend into shortening mixture. Chill dough at least 1 hour or until firm enough to handle.

Preheat oven to 350°F. Lightly grease cookie sheets. Beat egg white slightly. Shape dough into 1-inch balls. Dip each ball into egg white; roll in pecans to coat. Place 1 inch apart on prepared cookie sheet. Press thumb gently in center of each ball. Bake 10 to 12 minutes or until set. While cookies bake, prepare Caramel Filling. Press center of each cookie again with thumb to make indentation. Immediately spoon about ½ teaspoon Caramel Filling in center of each cookie. Carefully remove to wire racks to cool completely.

In small microwave-safe bowl, combine chocolate chips and shortening. Microwave at HIGH (100% power) 1 minute or until softened; stir. Allow to stand several minutes to finish melting; stir until smooth. Place waxed paper under wire racks with cookies. Drizzle chocolate mixture over top of cookies.   *Makes about 2 dozen cookies*

Caramel Filling: In small saucepan, combine 14 unwrapped light caramels and 3 tablespoons whipping cream. Cook over low heat, stirring frequently, until caramels are melted and mixture is smooth.

CHOCOLATE–DIPPED OAT COOKIES

2 cups uncooked rolled oats
¾ cup packed brown sugar
½ cup vegetable oil
½ cup finely chopped walnuts
1 egg

2 teaspoons grated orange peel
¼ teaspoon salt
1 package (11½ ounces) milk
chocolate chips

Combine oats, sugar, oil, walnuts, egg, orange peel and salt in large bowl until blended. Cover; refrigerate overnight. Preheat oven to 350°F. Lightly grease cookie sheets or line with parchment paper. Melt chocolate chips in top of double boiler over hot, not boiling, water; set aside. Shape oat mixture into large marble-sized balls. Place 2 inches apart on prepared cookie sheets. Bake 10 to 12 minutes or until golden and crisp. Cool 10 minutes on wire racks. Dip tops of cookies, one at a time, into melted chocolate. Place on waxed paper; cool until chocolate is set.   *Makes about 6 dozen cookies*

OATS 'N' PUMPKIN PINWHEELS

1½ cups sugar, divided
½ cup (1 stick) margarine, softened
2 egg whites
1½ cups all-purpose flour
1 cup QUAKER® Oats (Quick or Old
    Fashioned), uncooked

¼ teaspoon baking soda
1 cup canned pumpkin
½ teaspoon pumpkin pie spice
¼ cup sesame seeds

Beat 1 cup sugar and margarine until light and fluffy; mix in egg whites. Stir in combined flour, oats and baking soda. On waxed paper, press into 16×12-inch rectangle. Spread combined pumpkin, remaining ½ cup sugar and spice over dough to ½ inch from edge. From narrow end, roll up dough. Sprinkle sesame seeds around roll, pressing gently. Wrap in waxed paper; freeze overnight or until firm.

Preheat oven to 400°F. Spray cookie sheets with no-stick cooking spray. Cut frozen dough into ¼-inch slices; place 1 inch apart on prepared cookie sheets.

Bake 9 to 11 minutes or until golden brown. Remove to wire racks; cool completely.

Makes about 4 dozen cookies

CHOCOLATE–DIPPED ALMOND CRESCENTS

One end of these crescent-shaped cookies is dipped into melted chocolate—a decorative touch that makes them look special.

1 cup butter or margarine, softened
1 cup powdered sugar
2 egg yolks
2½ cups all-purpose flour

1½ teaspoons almond extract
1 cup (6 ounces) semisweet chocolate
    chips

Preheat oven to 375°F. Line cookie sheets with parchment paper or leave ungreased. Beat butter, sugar and egg yolks in large bowl. Beat in flour and almond extract until well mixed. Shape dough into 1-inch balls. (If dough is too soft to handle, cover and refrigerate until firm.) Roll balls into 2-inch long ropes, tapering both ends. Curve ropes into crescent shapes. Place 2 inches apart on prepared cookie sheets.

Bake 8 to 10 minutes or until set, but not browned. Remove to wire racks to cool. Melt chocolate chips in top of double boiler over hot, not boiling, water. Dip one end of each crescent in melted chocolate. Place on waxed paper; cool until chocolate is set.

Makes about 5 dozen cookies

Caramel Lace Chocolate Chip Cookies

CARAMEL LACE CHOCOLATE CHIP COOKIES

¼ cup BUTTER FLAVOR* CRISCO®
   All-Vegetable Shortening
½ cup light corn syrup
1 tablespoon brown sugar
½ teaspoon vanilla
1½ teaspoons grated orange peel
   (optional)

½ cup all-purpose flour
¼ teaspoon salt
⅓ cup semi-sweet chocolate chips
⅓ cup coarsely chopped pecans

1. Heat oven to 375°F. Grease baking sheets.

2. Combine shortening, corn syrup, brown sugar, vanilla and orange peel in large bowl. Beat at medium speed of electric mixer until well blended.

3. Combine flour and salt in small bowl. Mix into shortening mixture at low speed until blended. Stir in chocolate chips and pecans.

4. Drop teaspoonfuls of dough 4 inches apart onto prepared baking sheets.

5. Bake at 375°F for 5 minutes or until edges are golden brown. (Chips and nuts will remain in center while dough spreads out.) *Do not overbake.* Cool 2 minutes on baking sheets. Lift cookie edge with edge of spatula. Grasp cookie edge gently and lightly pinch or flute the edge, bringing it up to the chips and pecans in center. Work around each cookie until completely fluted. Remove to wire racks to cool completely.
Makes about 3 dozen cookies

*BUTTER FLAVOR CRISCO® is artificially flavored.

*Clockwise from top right: **Chocolate Mint Pinwheels** (page 106); **Chocolate Raspberry Linzer Cookies** (page 108); **New Wave Chocolate Spritz Cookies** (page 108)*

Homemade

HOLIDAY COOKIES

Holiday Favorites   84

Chips 'n' Chocolate   98

From the Cookie Jar   118

Brownies & Bars   132

Fanciful Cookies   146

Holiday Favorites

Baking a batch of these delightful cookies will fill your home with holiday cheer.

GLAZED SUGAR COOKIES

COOKIES
1 package DUNCAN HINES® Golden
   Sugar Cookie Mix

1 egg

GLAZE
1 cup sifted confectioners' sugar
1 to 2 tablespoons water or milk
½ teaspoon vanilla extract

Food coloring (optional)
Red and green sugar crystals,
   nonpareils or cinnamon candies

1. Preheat oven to 375°F.

2. **For cookies,** combine cookie mix, contents of buttery flavor packet from Mix and egg in large bowl. Stir until thoroughly blended. Roll dough to ⅛-inch thickness on lightly floured surface. Cut dough into desired shapes using floured cookie cutters. Place cookies 2 inches apart on ungreased baking sheets. Bake at 375°F for 5 to 6 minutes or until edges are light golden brown. Cool 1 minute on baking sheets. Remove to cooling racks. Cool completely.

3. **For glaze,** combine confectioners' sugar, water and vanilla extract in small bowl. Beat until smooth. Tint glaze with food coloring, if desired. Brush glaze on each cookie with clean pastry brush. Sprinkle cookies with sugar crystals, nonpareils or cinnamon candies before glaze sets. Allow glaze to set before storing between layers of waxed paper in airtight container. *Makes 2½ to 3 dozen cookies*

Glazed Sugar Cookies

Peanut Butter Reindeer

PEANUT BUTTER REINDEER

COOKIES
1 package DUNCAN HINES® Peanut
   Butter Cookie Mix

1 egg
2 teaspoons all-purpose flour

ASSORTED DECORATIONS
Miniature semi-sweet chocolate
   chips
Vanilla milk chips

Candy-coated semi-sweet chocolate
   chips
Colored sprinkles

1. **For cookies,** combine cookie mix, contents of peanut butter packet from Mix and egg in large bowl. Stir until thoroughly blended. Form dough into ball. Place flour in jumbo (15×13-inch) resealable plastic bag. Place ball of dough in bag. Shake to coat with flour. Place dough in center of bag (do not seal). Roll dough with rolling pin out to edges of bag. Slide bag onto baking sheet. Chill in refrigerator at least 1 hour.

2. Preheat oven to 375°F. Use scissors to cut bag down center and across ends. Turn plastic back to uncover dough. Dip reindeer cookie cutter in flour. Cut dough with reindeer cookie cutter. Dip cookie cutter in flour after each cut. Transfer cutout cookies to ungreased baking sheets using floured pancake turner. Decorate each reindeer as desired. Bake at 375°F for 5 to 7 minutes or until set but not browned. Cool 2 minutes on baking sheets. Remove to cooling racks. Cool completely. Store between layers of waxed paper in airtight container.   *Makes about 2 dozen cookies*

Tip: Reroll dough by folding plastic back over dough.

SANTA'S THUMBPRINTS

1 cup (2 sticks) margarine, softened
½ cup firmly packed brown sugar
1 whole egg or egg white
1 teaspoon vanilla
1½ cups QUAKER® Oats (Quick or Old
   Fashioned), uncooked

1½ cups all-purpose flour
1 cup finely chopped nuts
⅓ cup jelly or preserves

Heat oven to 350°F. Beat margarine and sugar in large bowl until light and fluffy. Blend in egg and vanilla. In large bowl, combine oats and flour; add to margarine mixture. Mix well. Shape into 1-inch balls; roll in chopped nuts. Place 2 inches apart on ungreased cookie sheet. Make indentation in center of each ball with thumb. Fill each thumbprint with about ¼ teaspoon jelly. Bake 12 to 15 minutes or until light golden brown. Cool completely on wire rack. Store loosely covered.   *Makes about 3 dozen cookies*

LINZER TARTS

1 cup BLUE BONNET® Margarine, softened
1 cup granulated sugar
2 cups all-purpose flour
1 cup PLANTERS® Slivered Almonds, chopped

1 teaspoon grated lemon peel
¼ teaspoon ground cinnamon
⅓ cup raspberry preserves
  Confectioners' sugar

In large bowl with electric mixer at high speed, beat margarine and granulated sugar until light and fluffy. Stir in flour, almonds, lemon peel and cinnamon until blended. Cover; chill 2 hours.

Divide dough in half. On floured surface, roll out one half of dough to ⅛-inch thickness. Using 2½-inch round cookie cutter, cut circles from dough. Reroll scraps to make additional rounds. Cut out ½-inch circles from centers of half the rounds. Repeat with remaining dough. Place on ungreased baking sheets. Bake at 325°F for 12 to 15 minutes or until lightly browned. Remove from sheets; cool on wire racks. Spread preserves on top of whole cookies. Top with cutout cookies to make sandwiches. Dust with confectioners' sugar.

Makes 2 dozen cookies

YULETIDE GINGER COOKIES

¾ cup firmly packed brown sugar
½ cup light corn syrup
½ cup (1 stick) margarine, softened
2 egg whites, slightly beaten
3 cups QUAKER® Oat Bran Hot Cereal, uncooked

¾ cup all-purpose flour
2 teaspoons ground ginger
1 teaspoon baking soda
1 teaspoon ground cinnamon
¼ cup red or green colored sugar crystals

Heat oven to 350°F. Beat brown sugar, corn syrup and margarine in medium bowl until fluffy. Blend in egg whites. In large bowl, combine oat bran, flour, ginger, baking soda and cinnamon. Gradually add brown sugar mixture; mix well. Shape into 1-inch balls; roll in colored sugar crystals to coat. Place 2 inches apart on ungreased cookie sheet. Gently press balls into 2-inch circles. Bake 11 to 13 minutes or until light golden brown. Cool 2 minutes on cookie sheet; remove to wire rack. Cool completely. Store tightly covered.

Makes about 3½ dozen cookies

HOLIDAY ALMOND WREATHS

¾ cup FLEISCHMANN'S® Margarine,
   softened
½ cup sugar
¼ cup EGG BEATERS® 99% Real Egg
   Product, thawed

1 teaspoon almond extract
2 cups all-purpose flour
½ cup ground PLANTERS® Almonds
   Green and red candied cherries
   (optional)

In medium bowl with electric mixer at medium speed, beat margarine and sugar until light and fluffy. Add egg product and almond extract; beat well. Stir in flour and ground almonds. Using pastry bag with ½-inch star tip, pipe dough into 1½-inch wreaths, 2 inches apart, onto ungreased baking sheets. Decorate wreaths with green and red candied cherries, if desired. Bake at 400°F for 10 to 12 minutes or until golden brown. Cool on wire racks.   *Makes 3 dozen cookies*

SUGAR COOKIES

1¼ cups granulated sugar
1 cup BUTTER FLAVOR* CRISCO®
   All-Vegetable Shortening
2 eggs
¼ cup light corn syrup or regular
   pancake syrup

1 tablespoon vanilla
3 cups plus 4 tablespoons
   all-purpose flour, divided
¾ teaspoon baking powder
½ teaspoon baking soda
½ teaspoon salt

1. Combine sugar and shortening in large bowl. Beat at medium speed of electric mixer until well blended. Add eggs, corn syrup and vanilla. Beat until light and fluffy.

2. In large bowl, combine 3 cups flour, baking powder, baking soda and salt; gradually add to sugar mixture at low speed. Mix until well blended. Divide dough into 4 quarters. Cover and refrigerate at least two hours or overnight.

3. Heat oven to 375°F.

4. Spread 1 tablespoon flour on large sheet of waxed paper. Place one quarter of dough on floured paper. Flatten slightly with hands. Turn dough over. Cover with another large sheet of waxed paper. Roll dough to ¼-inch thickness. Remove top layer of waxed paper. Cut out with cookie cutters. Place 2 inches apart on ungreased baking sheets. Roll and cut out remaining dough.

5. Bake at 375°F for 5 to 9 minutes, depending on size of cookies. (Bake smaller, thinner cookies 5 minutes; larger cookies 9 minutes.) Cool 2 minutes on baking sheets. Remove to wire racks to cool completely.   *Makes 3 to 4 dozen cookies*

Hint: Floured pastry cloth and rolling pin cover make rolling out dough easier.

*BUTTER FLAVOR CRISCO® is artificially flavored.

SPICED BANANA COOKIE WREATHS

2 extra-ripe, medium DOLE®
   Bananas, peeled
2 cups granola
1½ cups all-purpose flour
1 cup brown sugar, packed
1 teaspoon baking powder
1 teaspoon ground cinnamon
½ teaspoon ground nutmeg
¼ teaspoon salt

1 egg
½ cup margarine, melted
¼ cup vegetable oil
1 cup DOLE® Raisins
⅓ cup chopped DOLE® Almonds
½ cup powdered sugar
1 tablespoon milk
   Candied cherries or colored sugar
   crystals (optional)

• Place bananas in blender. Process until puréed; use 1 cup for recipe.

• Combine granola, flour, brown sugar, baking powder, cinnamon, nutmeg and salt in large bowl. Beat in 1 cup banana, egg, margarine and oil. Stir in raisins. For each of 3 wreaths, arrange about 16 generous teaspoonfuls dough with sides touching into a ring on greased cookie sheet. Sprinkle with almonds.

• Bake in 375°F oven 15 to 18 minutes until lightly browned. Cool on baking sheets.

• Combine powdered sugar and milk in small bowl until smooth. Drizzle over cooled wreaths. Decorate with candied cherries, if desired. Tie with a bow to give as a gift.

Makes 3 wreaths (16 cookies per wreath)

SNOW–COVERED ALMOND CRESCENTS

1 cup (2 sticks) margarine or butter,
   softened
¾ cup powdered sugar
½ teaspoon almond extract *or*
   2 teaspoons vanilla extract
2 cups all-purpose flour

¼ teaspoon salt (optional)
1 cup QUAKER® Oats (Quick or Old
   Fashioned), uncooked
½ cup finely chopped almonds
   Additional powdered sugar

Heat oven to 325°F. Beat margarine, ¾ cup powdered sugar and almond extract until light and fluffy. Add flour and salt; mix until well blended. Stir in oats and almonds. Using level measuring tablespoonfuls, shape dough into crescents. Bake on ungreased cookie sheets 14 to 17 minutes or until bottoms are light golden brown. Remove to wire racks. Sift additional powdered sugar generously over warm cookies. Cool completely.

Makes about 4 dozen cookies

RICHEST SPRITZ

1¼ cups confectioners' sugar	**½ teaspoon almond extract (optional)**
1 cup butter, softened	**2½ cups all-purpose flour**
2 egg yolks *or* 1 whole egg	**½ teaspoon salt**
1 teaspoon vanilla extract	**Food color (optional)**

Preheat oven to 400°F. Beat confectioners' sugar and butter in large bowl with electric mixer at medium speed. Beat in egg yolks, vanilla and almond extract. Combine flour and salt in medium bowl. Add to butter mixture; blend well. Tint dough with food color, if desired. Place dough in cookie press fitted with plate. Press onto ungreased cookie sheets, about 2 inches apart. Decorate as desired. Bake 6 to 8 minutes or until very slightly browned around edges. Remove to wire racks to cool.

Makes about 6½ dozen cookies

Spiced Banana Cookie Wreath

Milk Chocolate Florentine Cookies

MILK CHOCOLATE FLORENTINE COOKIES

⅔ cup butter or margarine
2 cups quick oats, uncooked
1 cup sugar
⅔ cup all-purpose flour
¼ cup corn syrup
¼ cup milk

1 teaspoon vanilla extract
¼ teaspoon salt
2 cups (12-ounce package) NESTLÉ®
   Toll House® Milk Chocolate
   Morsels

Preheat oven to 375°F.

Melt butter in medium saucepan over low heat. Remove from heat. Stir in oats, sugar, flour, corn syrup, milk, vanilla extract and salt; mix well. Drop by measuring teaspoonfuls, about 3 inches apart, onto foil-lined cookie sheets. Spread thin with rubber spatula.

Bake 5 to 7 minutes. Cool on cookie sheets. Peel foil away from cookies.

Melt morsels over hot, not boiling, water; stir until smooth. Spread chocolate on flat side of half the cookies. Top with remaining cookies. *Makes 3½ dozen sandwich cookies*

SUGAR COOKIE ORNAMENTS

1 package DUNCAN HINES® Golden Sugar Cookie Mix
1 egg
1 teaspoon milk
Assorted colored sugar crystals, cinnamon gems, nonpareils or decors

DUNCAN HINES® Creamy Homestyle Vanilla Frosting (optional)

1. Preheat oven to 375°F.

2. Combine cookie mix, contents of buttery flavor packet from Mix, egg and milk in large bowl. Stir until thoroughly blended. Form dough into 1-inch balls. Place 3 inches apart on ungreased baking sheets. Grease and flour bottom of drinking glass. Press gently to flatten cookies to form 2-inch circles.

3. Press end of drinking straw into top of each cookie to make hole. Decorate cookies as desired or leave plain to frost.

4. Bake at 375°F for 5 to 7 minutes or until set but not browned. Press straw through holes in top of cookies again. Cool 1 minute on baking sheets. Remove to cooling racks. Cool completely. Frost plain cookies, if desired.

5. String ribbon through holes in cookies. Tie at top.   *Makes 3½ to 4 dozen cookies*

Tip: Frosting can be divided and tinted with a few drops of red and green food coloring. Stir until well blended. Frost patterns on ornaments or frost and sprinkle with decors.

Painted Ornaments: Combine 1 egg yolk and 1 teaspoon water. Stir well. Divide into 3 custard cups. Tint each with 1 drop of different food coloring. Sketch design on unbaked cookie with tip of knife. Use clean watercolor paintbrushes to paint designs on cookies before baking. Bake and cool as directed.

ANISE PILLOWS
PFEFFERNEUSSE

1⅔ cups all-purpose flour
1½ teaspoons DAVIS® Baking Powder
½ teaspoon grated lemon peel
¼ teaspoon salt
¼ teaspoon ground cinnamon
¼ teaspoon ground nutmeg
⅛ teaspoon ground cloves
⅛ teaspoon white pepper
⅓ cup BLUE BONNET® Margarine, softened

½ cup granulated sugar
1 egg
½ cup milk
½ cup PLANTERS® Walnuts, finely chopped
½ teaspoon anise seed
Confectioners' sugar

In small bowl, combine flour, baking powder, lemon peel, salt, cinnamon, nutmeg, cloves and white pepper; set aside. In large bowl, beat together margarine and granulated sugar until creamy; beat in egg. Add flour mixture alternately with milk, beating well after each addition. Stir in walnuts and anise seed. Drop dough by teaspoonfuls, 2 inches apart, onto lightly greased baking sheets.

Bake at 350°F for 15 to 17 minutes. Cool slightly on wire racks. Roll in confectioners' sugar while still warm; cool completely.
Makes 5 dozen cookies

OATMEAL–BANANA LEBKUCHEN

¾ cup margarine, softened
½ cup brown sugar, packed
¼ cup honey
1½ teaspoons ground cinnamon
1½ teaspoons ground ginger
1 teaspoon ground cardamom
½ teaspoon ground cloves
2 extra-ripe, medium DOLE® Bananas, peeled

2 eggs, beaten
1¾ cups all-purpose flour
½ teaspoon baking powder
½ teaspoon baking soda
½ teaspoon salt
¾ cup DOLE® Chopped Almonds
½ cup mixed candied fruit, finely chopped
2 cups quick oats, uncooked

LEMON GLAZE
¾ cup sifted powdered sugar
Juice from 1 DOLE® Lemon (1 tablespoon)

1 drop almond extract

- Beat margarine, brown sugar and honey in large bowl. Beat in cinnamon, ginger, cardamom and cloves.

- Mash bananas with fork in small bowl; use 1 cup for recipe. Add 1 cup banana and eggs to margarine mixture; beat until blended.

- Combine flour, baking powder, baking soda and salt in small bowl. Stir in almonds and candied fruit. Add to margarine mixture. Stir until well blended. Stir in oats.

- Drop by heaping teaspoonfuls, 2 inches apart, onto greased cookie sheets. Bake in 400°F oven 8 minutes. Cool completely on wire racks. Spread with Lemon Glaze or dust with powdered sugar. When glaze has set, store cookies in airtight container. *Makes 4 dozen cookies*

Lemon Glaze: Combine all ingredients until blended.

CHRISTMAS TREASURE NUGGETS

1 cup (2 sticks) margarine or butter, softened
1 cup firmly packed brown sugar
¾ cup granulated sugar
2 eggs
1 teaspoon vanilla
1¾ cups all-purpose flour
1 teaspoon baking soda

½ teaspoon baking powder
½ teaspoon salt (optional)
2 cups QUAKER® Oats (Quick or Old Fashioned), uncooked
2 cups QUAKER® 100% Natural Cereal, any flavor
Whole blanched almonds

Heat oven to 375°F. Beat margarine and sugars in large bowl until light and fluffy. Blend in eggs and vanilla. In medium bowl, combine flour, baking soda, baking powder and salt; add to margarine mixture; mix well. Stir in oats and cereal.

Drop by rounded teaspoonfuls, 2 inches apart, onto ungreased cookie sheet. Press 1 almond onto each cookie. Bake 8 to 10 minutes or until golden brown. Cool 2 minutes on cookie sheet; remove to wire rack. Cool completely. Store tightly covered. *Makes 6 dozen cookies*

Sugar Cookie Wreaths

SUGAR COOKIE WREATHS

1 package DUNCAN HINES® Golden
   Sugar Cookie Mix
1 egg

Green food coloring
Candied or maraschino cherry
   pieces

1. Preheat oven to 375°F. Combine cookie mix, contents of buttery flavor packet from Mix and egg in large bowl. Stir until thoroughly blended.

2. Tint dough with green food coloring. Stir until desired color. Form into balls the size of miniature marshmallows. For each wreath, arrange 9 or 10 balls with sides touching into a ring on ungreased baking sheet. Flatten slightly with fingers. Place small piece of candied cherry on each ball.

3. Bake at 375°F for 5 to 7 minutes or until set but not browned. Cool 1 minute on baking sheets. Remove to cooling racks. Cool completely. Store in airtight container.   *Makes 2 dozen cookies*

STAINED GLASS COOKIES

½ cup BLUE BONNET® Margarine,
   softened
½ cup sugar
½ cup honey
1 egg
1 teaspoon vanilla extract

3 cups all-purpose flour
1 teaspoon DAVIS® Baking Powder
½ teaspoon baking soda
½ teaspoon salt
5 rolls LIFE SAVERS® Fancy Fruits
   Candy

In large bowl with electric mixer at medium speed, beat margarine, sugar, honey, egg and vanilla extract until thoroughly blended. Blend in flour, baking powder, baking soda and salt. Cover; chill in refrigerator at least 2 hours.

On lightly floured surface, roll out dough to ¼-inch thickness. Cut dough with cookie cutters into desired shapes. Trace smaller version of cookie shape on dough leaving a ½- to ¾-inch border of dough. Cut out and remove dough from center of cookies. Place cookie outlines on baking sheets lined with foil.

Crush each color of candy separately between two layers of waxed paper with mallet. Spoon crushed candy inside centers of cookies.

Bake at 350°F for 6 to 8 minutes or until candy is melted and cookie is lightly browned. Cool cookies completely before removing from foil.   *Makes 3½ dozen cookies*

Chips 'n' Chocolate

Chocolate in every flavor and form is evident in this chapter—white, dark and milk chocolate in chips, glazes, fillings and more!

CHOCOLATE CHIPS THUMBPRINT COOKIES

1 cup HERSHEY®'S Semi-Sweet
  Chocolate Chips, divided
¼ cup butter or margarine, softened
¼ cup shortening
½ cup sugar

1 egg, separated
½ teaspoon vanilla extract
1 cup all-purpose flour
¼ teaspoon salt
1 cup finely chopped nuts

Heat oven to 350°F. In small microwave-safe bowl, place ¼ cup chocolate chips. Microwave at HIGH (100% power) 20 to 30 seconds or just until chocolate is melted and smooth when stirred; set aside to cool slightly. In large mixer bowl, combine butter, shortening, sugar, reserved melted chocolate, egg yolk and vanilla; blend well. Stir in flour and salt. Roll dough into 1-inch balls. With fork, slightly beat egg white. Dip each ball into egg white; roll in chopped nuts. Place balls on ungreased cookie sheet, about 1 inch apart. Press center of each ball with thumb to make indentation. Bake 10 to 12 minutes or until set. Remove from oven; immediately place several of remaining ¾ cup chocolate chips in center of each cookie. Carefully remove from cookie sheet to wire rack. After several minutes, swirl melted chocolate in each thumbprint. Cool completely.

Makes about 2½ dozen cookies

Chocolate Chips Thumbprint Cookies

White Chocolate Biggies; Peanut Butter Jumbos

WHITE CHOCOLATE BIGGIES

1½ cups butter or margarine, softened
1 cup granulated sugar
¾ cup packed light brown sugar
2 teaspoons vanilla
2 eggs
2½ cups all-purpose flour
⅔ cup unsweetened cocoa

1 teaspoon baking soda
½ teaspoon salt
1 package (10 ounces) large white chocolate chips
¾ cup pecan halves, coarsely chopped
½ cup golden raisins

Preheat oven to 350°F. Lightly grease cookie sheets or line with parchment paper. Beat butter, sugars, vanilla and eggs in large bowl until light and fluffy. Combine flour, cocoa, baking soda and salt in medium bowl; blend into butter mixture until smooth. Stir in white chocolate chips, pecans and raisins. Scoop out about ⅓ cup dough for each cookie. Place on prepared cookie sheets, about 4 inches apart. Flatten each cookie slightly. Bake 12 to 14 minutes or until firm in center. Cool 5 minutes on cookie sheets; remove to wire racks to cool completely.

Makes about 2 dozen large cookies

PEANUT BUTTER JUMBOS

1½ cups peanut butter
½ cup butter or margarine, softened
1 cup packed brown sugar
1 cup granulated sugar
3 eggs
2 tablespoons baking soda

1 teaspoon vanilla
4½ cups rolled oats, uncooked
1 cup (6 ounces) semisweet
   chocolate chips
1 cup candy-coated chocolate pieces

Preheat oven to 350°F. Lightly grease cookie sheets or line with parchment paper. Beat peanut butter, butter, sugars and eggs in large bowl until light and fluffy. Blend in baking soda, vanilla and oats until well mixed. Stir in chocolate chips and candy pieces. Scoop out about ⅓ cup dough for each cookie. Place on prepared cookie sheets, about 4 inches apart. Flatten each cookie slightly. Bake 15 to 20 minutes or until firm in center. Remove to wire racks to cool completely.

Makes about 1½ dozen large cookies

ALMOND DOUBLE CHIP COOKIES

¾ cup butter or margarine, softened
¾ cup packed light brown sugar
1 egg
½ teaspoon almond extract
1½ cups all-purpose flour
¼ teaspoon baking soda

Dash salt
1 cup (6 ounces) semisweet
   chocolate chips
1 cup (6 ounces) vanilla milk chips
½ cup slivered blanched almonds

Preheat oven to 375°F. Line cookie sheets with parchment paper or leave ungreased. Beat butter and brown sugar in large bowl until creamy. Beat in egg and almond extract. Combine flour, baking soda and salt in small bowl. Blend into butter mixture. Stir in semisweet and vanilla milk chips and almonds. Drop dough by rounded tablespoonfuls, 3 inches apart, onto prepared cookie sheets. Bake 8 to 10 minutes or until light brown. *Do not overbake.* Cool 2 minutes on cookie sheets; remove to wire racks to cool completely.

Makes about 3 dozen cookies

CHOCOLATE SUGAR COOKIES

3 squares BAKER'S® Unsweetened
   Chocolate
1 cup (2 sticks) margarine or butter
1 cup sugar
1 egg

1 teaspoon vanilla
2 cups all-purpose flour
1 teaspoon baking soda
¼ teaspoon salt
Additional sugar

Microwave chocolate and margarine in large microwavable bowl on HIGH (100% power) 2 minutes or until margarine is melted. Stir until chocolate is completely melted.

Stir 1 cup sugar into chocolate mixture until well blended. Stir in egg and vanilla until completely blended. Mix in flour, baking soda and salt. Refrigerate 30 minutes.

Heat oven to 375°F. Shape dough into 1-inch balls; roll in additional sugar. Place, 2 inches apart, on ungreased cookie sheets. (If flatter, crisper cookies are desired, flatten balls with bottom of drinking glass.)

Bake 8 to 10 minutes or until set. Remove from cookie sheets to cool on wire racks.

Makes about 3½ dozen cookies

Prep time: 15 minutes
Chill time: 30 minutes
Baking time: 8 to 10 minutes

Jam-Filled Chocolate Sugar Cookies: Prepare Chocolate Sugar Cookie dough as directed. Roll in finely chopped nuts in place of sugar. Make indentation in each ball; fill center with your favorite jam. Bake as directed.

Chocolate-Caramel Sugar Cookies: Prepare Chocolate Sugar Cookie dough as directed. Roll in finely chopped nuts in place of sugar. Make indentation in each ball; bake as directed. Microwave 1 package (14 ounces) KRAFT® Caramels with 2 tablespoons milk in microwavable bowl on HIGH (100% power) 3 minutes or until melted, stirring after 2 minutes. Fill centers of cookies with caramel mixture. Drizzle with melted BAKER'S® Semi-Sweet Chocolate.

Top to bottom: Chocolate Sugar Cookies; Jam-Filled Chocolate Sugar Cookies; Chocolate-Caramel Sugar Cookies

Chocolate Chip Lollipops

CHOCOLATE CHIP LOLLIPOPS

1 package DUNCAN HINES®
    Chocolate Chip Cookie Mix
1 egg

2 teaspoons water
24 flat ice cream sticks
Assorted decors

1. Preheat oven to 375°F.

2. Combine cookie mix, buttery flavor packet from Mix, egg and water in large bowl. Stir until thoroughly blended. Shape dough into 24 (1-inch) balls. Place balls 3 inches apart on ungreased baking sheets. Push ice cream stick into center of each ball. Flatten each ball with hand to form round lollipop. Decorate by pressing decors onto dough.

3. Bake at 375°F for 8 to 9 minutes or until light golden brown. Cool 1 minute on baking sheets. Remove to cooling racks. Cool completely. Store in airtight container.   *Makes 2 dozen cookies*

Tip: For best results, use shiny baking sheets for baking cookies. Dark baking sheets cause cookie bottoms to become too brown.

MINT CHOCOLATE CHEWS

½ cup BLUE BONNET® Margarine
1 cup sugar
2 (1-ounce) squares unsweetened
    chocolate, melted
1 egg
⅓ cup buttermilk
1 teaspoon vanilla extract

1¾ cups all-purpose flour
½ teaspoon baking soda
¼ teaspoon salt
3 (.35-ounce) packages Pep-O-Mint
    LIFE SAVERS® Holes
½ cup walnuts, chopped

In large bowl with mixer at medium speed, beat margarine, sugar, melted chocolate and egg until creamy. Stir in buttermilk and vanilla until smooth. Mix in flour, baking soda and salt until blended; stir in holes and walnuts. Cover and chill dough at least 1 hour.

Drop dough by level tablespoonfuls, 2 inches apart, onto ungreased baking sheets. Bake at 400°F for 8 to 10 minutes or until set. Remove from sheets; cool on wire racks.   *Makes 3 dozen cookies*

CHOCOLATE MINT PINWHEELS

½ cup (from 6-ounce package)
NESTLÉ® Toll House® Mint
Flavored Semi-Sweet Chocolate
Morsels, divided
¾ cup (1½ sticks) butter, softened
⅓ cup sugar

½ teaspoon salt
1 egg
1 teaspoon vanilla extract
2¼ cups all-purpose flour

Over hot, not boiling, water, melt morsels, stirring until smooth. Cool to room temperature; set aside. In large mixer bowl, beat butter, sugar and salt until creamy. Beat in egg and vanilla extract.* Gradually add flour. Place 1 cup dough in medium bowl; blend in melted morsels. Shape chocolate dough and remaining dough into separate balls; flatten and cover with plastic wrap. Refrigerate until firm, about 1½ hours.

Preheat oven to 375°F. Between sheets of waxed paper, roll each ball of dough into a 13×9-inch rectangle. Remove top layers of waxed paper. Invert chocolate dough onto plain dough. Peel off remaining waxed paper. Starting with a long side, roll up, jelly-roll style. Cut into ¼-inch slices; place on ungreased cookie sheets.

Bake 7 to 10 minutes. Let stand on cookie sheets 2 minutes. Remove from cookie sheets; cool completely.

Makes 3½ dozen cookies

*Mixture may look curdled.

ALL–AMERICAN CHOCOLATE CHIP COOKIES

⅔ cup butter or margarine, softened
⅓ cup shortening
1 cup packed brown sugar
½ cup granulated sugar
1 egg
1 teaspoon vanilla

2 cups all-purpose flour
1 teaspoon baking soda
1 teaspoon salt
1 package (12 ounces) semisweet
chocolate chips
1 cup chopped walnuts

In large bowl, beat butter, shortening and sugars. Beat in egg and vanilla. Combine flour, baking soda and salt in small bowl; stir into butter mixture, mixing well. Stir in chocolate chips and nuts. Drop by teaspoonfuls, 2 inches apart, onto greased baking sheets. Bake in 350°F oven 8 to 10 minutes, just until edges are golden (centers will still be soft). Remove to wire racks to cool. *Makes about 3 dozen cookies*

Favorite recipe from Walnut Marketing Board

Clockwise from top right: Chocolate Mint Pinwheels; Chocolate Raspberry Linzer Cookies (page 108); New Wave Chocolate Spritz Cookies (page 108)

CHOCOLATE RASPBERRY LINZER COOKIES

2⅓ cups all-purpose flour
1 teaspoon baking powder
½ teaspoon cinnamon
½ teaspoon salt
1 cup granulated sugar
¾ cup (1½ sticks) butter, softened
2 eggs

½ teaspoon almond extract
2 cups (12-ounce package) NESTLÉ®
   Toll House® Semi-Sweet
   Chocolate Morsels
6 tablespoons raspberry jam or
   preserves
Confectioners' sugar

In small bowl, combine flour, baking powder, cinnamon and salt; set aside. In large mixer bowl, beat granulated sugar and butter until light and fluffy. Beat in eggs and almond extract. Gradually add flour mixture. Divide dough in half. Wrap in plastic wrap; refrigerate until firm.

Preheat oven to 350°F. On lightly floured board, roll out half of dough to ⅛-inch thickness. Cut with 2½-inch round cookie cutter. Repeat with remaining dough. Cut 1-inch-round centers from half of unbaked cookies. Place on ungreased cookie sheets. Reroll dough trimmings, if necessary.

Bake 8 to 10 minutes just until set. Let stand on cookie sheets 2 minutes. Remove from cookie sheets; cool completely.

Over hot, not boiling, water, melt morsels, stirring until smooth. Spread 1 measuring teaspoonful melted chocolate on flat side of each whole cookie. Top with ½ measuring teaspoonful raspberry jam. Sprinkle confectioners' sugar on cookies with center holes; place flat side down on top of chocolate-jam cookies to form cookie sandwiches.   *Makes about 3 dozen sandwich cookies*

NEW WAVE CHOCOLATE SPRITZ COOKIES

1 cup (6-ounce package) NESTLÉ®
   Toll House® Semi-Sweet
   Chocolate Morsels
1 cup (2 sticks) butter, softened
⅔ cup sugar

1 teaspoon vanilla extract
2 eggs
2½ cups all-purpose flour
1 jar (4 ounces) cinnamon candies

Over hot, not boiling, water, melt morsels, stirring until smooth; set aside.

In large mixer bowl, beat butter, sugar and vanilla extract until light and fluffy. Beat in eggs. Stir in melted morsels. Gradually beat in flour. Cover dough; refrigerate 30 to 45 minutes.

Preheat oven to 400°F. Place dough in cookie press fitted with star plate. Press dough into 2-inch circles on ungreased cookie sheets; decorate with cinnamon candies.

Bake 5 minutes or just until set. Let stand on cookie sheets 2 minutes. Remove from cookie sheets; cool completely.   *Makes about 7½ dozen cookies*

CHOCOLATE MINT SNOW–TOP COOKIES

1½ cups all-purpose flour
1½ teaspoons baking powder
¼ teaspoon salt
1½ cups (10-ounce package) NESTLÉ®
 Toll House® Mint Flavored
 Semi-Sweet Chocolate Morsels,
 divided

6 tablespoons (¾ stick) butter,
 softened
1 cup granulated sugar
1½ teaspoons vanilla extract
2 eggs
 Confectioners' sugar

In small bowl, combine flour, baking powder and salt; set aside. Over hot, not boiling, water, melt 1 cup morsels, stirring until smooth; set aside. In large mixer bowl, beat butter and granulated sugar until creamy. Add melted morsels and vanilla extract. Beat in eggs. Gradually beat in flour mixture. Stir in remaining ½ cup morsels. Wrap dough in plastic wrap and freeze until firm, about 20 minutes.

Preheat oven to 350°F. Shape dough into 1-inch balls; coat with confectioners' sugar. Place on ungreased cookie sheets. Bake 10 to 12 minutes until tops appear cracked. Let stand on cookie sheets 5 minutes. Remove from cookie sheets; cool completely.   *Makes about 3 dozen cookies*

KAHLÚA® MUDSLIDE BROWNIES

2 cups all-purpose flour
½ teaspoon baking powder
½ teaspoon salt
⅔ cup butter
4 squares (1 ounce *each*)
 unsweetened chocolate, chopped
3 eggs
1½ cups granulated sugar

4 tablespoons KAHLÚA®
2 tablespoons Irish cream liqueur
1 tablespoon vodka
¾ cup coarsely chopped walnuts
 (optional)
 Kahlúa® Glaze (recipe follows)
 Whole coffee beans (optional)

Combine flour, baking powder and salt in small bowl. Melt butter and chocolate in small saucepan over low heat; set aside. Beat eggs and granulated sugar in large bowl until light and fluffy. Beat in flour mixture, chocolate mixture, 4 tablespoons Kahlúa®, Irish cream and vodka. Fold in walnuts, if desired. Pour into greased 13×9-inch baking pan. Bake in 350°F oven just until toothpick inserted in center comes out clean, about 25 minutes. *Do not overbake.* Cool in pan on wire rack. Prepare Kahlúa® Glaze; spread with glaze. Decorate with whole coffee beans, if desired. Cut into squares.

Makes 24 brownies

KAHLÚA® GLAZE

1¼ cups powdered sugar   3 tablespoons KAHLÚA®

Beat together powdered sugar and 3 tablespoons Kahlúa® in small bowl until smooth.

ORIGINAL TOLL HOUSE® CHOCOLATE CHIP COOKIES

2¼ cups all-purpose flour
1 teaspoon baking soda
1 teaspoon salt
1 cup (2 sticks) butter, softened
¾ cup granulated sugar
¾ cup firmly packed brown sugar

2 eggs
1 teaspoon vanilla extract
2 cups (12-ounce package) NESTLÉ®
  Toll House® Semi-Sweet
  Chocolate Morsels
1 cup nuts, chopped

Preheat oven to 375°F. In small bowl, combine flour, baking soda and salt; set aside.

In large mixer bowl, beat butter, granulated sugar and brown sugar until creamy. Add eggs, 1 at a time, beating well after each addition. Blend in vanilla extract. Gradually beat in flour mixture. Stir in morsels and nuts. Drop by rounded measuring tablespoonfuls onto ungreased cookie sheets.

Bake 9 to 11 minutes until edges are golden brown. Let stand 2 minutes. Remove from cookie sheets; cool completely.

Makes about 5 dozen cookies

Toll House® Pan Cookies: Preheat oven to 375°F. Prepare dough as directed; spread in greased 15½×10½-inch baking pan. Bake 20 to 25 minutes until golden brown. Cool completely. Cut into 2-inch squares. Makes about 3 dozen cookies.

Refrigerator Toll House® Cookies: Prepare dough as directed. Divide dough in half; wrap halves separately in waxed paper. Refrigerate 1 hour or until firm. On waxed paper, shape each dough half into 15-inch log; wrap in waxed paper. Refrigerate 30 minutes.*

Preheat oven to 375°F. Cut each log into 30 (½-inch) slices. Place on ungreased cookie sheets. Bake 8 to 10 minutes until edges are golden brown. Makes about 5 dozen cookies.

*Dough may be stored up to 1 week in refrigerator or up to 8 weeks in freezer, if foil- or freezer-wrapped.

Original Toll House® Chocolate Chip Cookies

CHOCOLATE MINT SUGAR COOKIE DROPS

2½ cups all-purpose flour
1¼ teaspoons baking powder
¾ teaspoon salt
1 cup granulated sugar
¾ cup vegetable oil
2 eggs

1 teaspoon vanilla extract
1½ cups (10-ounce package) NESTLÉ®
   Toll House® Mint Flavored
   Semi-Sweet Chocolate Morsels
Assorted colored sugars or
   additional granulated sugar

Preheat oven to 350°F. In small bowl, combine flour, baking powder and salt; set aside.

In large mixer bowl, combine granulated sugar and oil. Add eggs, 1 at a time, beating well after each addition. Blend in vanilla extract. Gradually beat in flour mixture. Stir in morsels. Shape rounded measuring teaspoonfuls of dough into balls; roll in colored sugar. Place on ungreased cookie sheets.

Bake 8 to 10 minutes until set. Let stand on cookie sheets 2 minutes. Remove from cookie sheets; cool completely.
Makes about 5½ dozen cookies

Chocolate Mint Sugar Cookie Drops

CHOCOLATE MELTING MOMENTS

1 cup butter or margarine, softened
⅓ cup confectioners' sugar
¼ cup unsweetened cocoa

1½ cups cake flour
Mocha Filling (recipe follows)

Preheat oven to 350°F. Lightly grease cookie sheets or line with parchment paper. Beat 1 cup butter, ⅓ cup confectioners' sugar and cocoa in large bowl until light and fluffy. Blend in cake flour until smooth. Shape dough into marble-sized balls. (If dough is too soft to handle, cover and refrigerate until firm.) Place 2 inches apart on prepared cookie sheets. Press center of each ball with knuckle of finger to make indentation. Bake 10 to 12 minutes or until set. Remove to wire racks. Prepare Mocha Filling. While cookies are still warm, spoon about ½ teaspoonful filling into center of each.

Makes about 5 dozen cookies

MOCHA FILLING

1 tablespoon butter or margarine
1 square (1 ounce) unsweetened
  chocolate
1 cup confectioners' sugar

1 teaspoon vanilla
1 to 2 tablespoons hot coffee or
  water

Melt 1 tablespoon butter and chocolate in small heavy saucepan over low heat; stir until melted. Blend in 1 cup confectioners' sugar, vanilla and enough coffee to make smooth filling.

CHOCOLATE CREAM CHEESE SUGAR COOKIE BARS

1 package (15 ounces) golden sugar
  cookie mix
1 package (8 ounces) cream cheese,
  softened
¼ cup butter or margarine, softened

¼ cup HERSHEY®S Cocoa
½ cup granulated sugar
1 egg
1 teaspoon vanilla extract
Powdered sugar (optional)

Preheat oven to 350°F. Mix cookie dough according to package directions; spread in 9-inch square baking pan. In small mixer bowl, beat cream cheese and butter until light and fluffy. Stir together cocoa and granulated sugar in small bowl; add to cream cheese mixture. Add egg and vanilla; beat until smooth. Spread cream cheese mixture over cookie batter.

Bake 40 minutes or until no imprint remains when touched lightly. Cool completely in pan on wire rack. Sprinkle powdered sugar over top, if desired. Cut into bars. Cover; refrigerate.   *Makes about 16 bars*

CHOCOLATE LACE CORNUCOPIAS

½ cup firmly packed brown sugar
½ cup corn syrup
¼ cup (½ stick) margarine or butter
4 squares BAKER'S® Semi-Sweet
  Chocolate

1 cup all-purpose flour
1 cup finely chopped nuts
  Whipped cream or COOL WHIP®
  Whipped Topping, thawed

Heat oven to 350°F. Microwave brown sugar, corn syrup and margarine in large microwavable bowl on HIGH (100% power) 2 minutes or until boiling. Stir in chocolate squares until completely melted. Gradually stir in flour and nuts until well blended. Drop by level tablespoonfuls, 4 inches apart, onto foil-lined cookie sheets.

Bake 10 minutes. Lift foil and cookies onto wire racks. Cool 3 to 4 minutes or until cookies can be easily peeled off foil. Remove foil; finish cooling cookies on wire racks that have been covered with paper towels.

Place several cookies, lacy side down, on foil-lined cookie sheet. Heat at 350°F for 2 to 3 minutes or until slightly softened. Remove from foil, 1 at a time, and roll, lacy side out, to form cones. Cool completely. Just before serving, fill with whipped cream. *Makes about 30 cornucopias*

Prep time: 20 minutes
Baking time: 12 to 13 minutes

Saucepan preparation: Mix sugar, corn syrup and margarine in 2-quart saucepan. Bring to a boil over medium heat, stirring constantly. Remove from heat; stir in chocolate squares until completely melted. Continue as directed.

Chocolate Lace Cornucopias

Peanut Butter and Chocolate Cookie Sandwich Cookies

PEANUT BUTTER AND CHOCOLATE COOKIE SANDWICH COOKIES

½ cup REESE'S® Peanut Butter Chips
3 tablespoons plus ½ cup butter or
   margarine, softened and divided
1¼ cups sugar, divided
¼ cup light corn syrup
1 egg
1 teaspoon vanilla extract
2 cups plus 2 tablespoons all-purpose
   flour, divided

2 teaspoons baking soda
¼ teaspoon salt
½ cup HERSHEY'S Cocoa
5 tablespoons butter or margarine,
   melted
Additional sugar
About 2 dozen large marshmallows

Heat oven to 350°F. In small saucepan over very low heat, melt peanut butter chips and 3 tablespoons softened butter. Remove from heat; cool slightly. In large mixer bowl, beat remaining ½ cup softened butter and 1 cup sugar until light and fluffy. Add corn syrup, egg and vanilla; blend thoroughly. Combine 2 cups flour, baking soda and salt; add to butter mixture, blending well. Remove 1¼ cups batter and place in small bowl; with wooden spoon, stir in remaining 2 tablespoons flour and peanut butter chip mixture. Blend cocoa, remaining ¼ cup sugar and melted butter into remaining batter. Refrigerate both batters 5 to 10 minutes or until firm enough to handle.

Roll both doughs into 1-inch balls; roll in additional sugar. Place on ungreased cookie sheet. Bake 10 to 11 minutes or until set. Cool slightly; remove from cookie sheet to wire rack. Cool completely. Place 1 marshmallow on flat side of 1 chocolate cookie. Microwave at MEDIUM (50% power) 10 seconds or until marshmallow is softened. Place a peanut butter cookie over marshmallow, pressing down slightly. Repeat with remaining marshmallows and cookies. Serve immediately.

Makes about 2 dozen sandwich cookies

NUTTY CHOCOLATE STARS

¾ cup (1½ sticks) margarine or
    butter, softened
¾ cup firmly packed brown sugar
1 egg
1 teaspoon vanilla
3 cups QUAKER® Oats (Quick or Old
    Fashioned), uncooked

1 cup all-purpose flour
½ teaspoon baking soda
⅔ cup finely chopped nuts
One 6- to 7-ounce package milk
    chocolate candy stars or
    kisses

Heat oven to 350°F. Lightly grease cookie sheet. Beat margarine and sugar until light and fluffy. Blend in egg and vanilla. In large bowl, combine oats, flour and baking soda; add to margarine mixture. Mix well. Shape into 1-inch balls; roll in nuts. Place on prepared cookie sheet. Bake 10 to 12 minutes or until light golden brown. Remove from oven; gently press chocolate candy into center of each cookie. Cool 2 minutes on cookie sheet; remove to wire rack. Cool completely. Store tightly covered.

Makes 3½ dozen cookies

Notes:
Dough may be covered and stored in the refrigerator for up to two days.
Candied cherries may be substituted for chocolate candy, if desired.

From the Cookie Jar

It won't be easy to keep the cookie jar full with these fabulous favorites.

PEANUT BUTTER SPRITZ SANDWICHES

1 package DUNCAN HINES® Peanut
  Butter Cookie Mix
1 egg

3 bars (1.55 ounces each) milk
  chocolate

1. Preheat oven to 375°F.

2. Combine cookie mix, contents of peanut butter packet from Mix and egg in large bowl. Stir until thoroughly blended. Fill cookie press with dough. Press desired shapes 2 inches apart onto ungreased baking sheets. Bake at 375°F for 7 to 9 minutes or until set but not browned. Cool 1 minute on baking sheets.

3. Cut each milk chocolate bar into 12 sections by following division marks on bars.

4. To assemble, carefully remove 1 cookie from baking sheet. Place 1 milk chocolate section on bottom of warm cookie; top with second cookie. Press together to make sandwich. Repeat with remaining cookies. Place sandwich cookies on cooling racks until chocolate is set. Store in airtight container.

Makes 2½ to 3 dozen sandwich cookies

Tip: For best appearance, use cookie press plates that give solid shapes.

Peanut Butter Spritz Sandwiches

Pineapple-Raisin Jumbles

PINEAPPLE–RAISIN JUMBLES

2 cans (8 ounces each) DOLE®
    Crushed Pineapple in Juice
½ cup margarine, softened
½ cup sugar
1 teaspoon vanilla extract
1 cup all-purpose flour

4 teaspoons grated DOLE® Orange
    peel
1 cup DOLE® Blanched Slivered
    Almonds, toasted
1 cup DOLE® Raisins

• Drain pineapple well, pressing out excess liquid with back of spoon. Reserve juice for beverage.

• Beat margarine and sugar in large bowl until light and fluffy. Stir in drained pineapple and vanilla. Beat in flour and orange peel. Stir in almonds and raisins.

• Drop by heaping tablespoonfuls, 2 inches apart, onto greased cookie sheets.

• Bake in 350°F oven 20 to 22 minutes until firm. Cool on wire racks.   *Makes 2 to 2½ dozen cookies*

CHUNKY BUTTER CHRISTMAS COOKIES

1¼ cups butter, softened
1 cup packed brown sugar
½ cup dairy sour cream
1 egg
2 teaspoons vanilla
1½ cups all-purpose flour
1 teaspoon baking soda
1 teaspoon salt

1½ cups old-fashioned or quick oats, uncooked
1 package (10 ounces) vanilla milk chips
1 cup flaked coconut
1 jar (3½ ounces) macadamia nuts, coarsely chopped

Beat butter and brown sugar in large bowl until light and fluffy. Blend in sour cream, egg and vanilla. Combine flour, baking soda and salt in small bowl. Add to butter mixture; mix well. Stir in oats, vanilla milk chips, coconut and nuts. Drop rounded teaspoonfuls of dough, 2 inches apart, onto ungreased cookie sheets.

Bake at 375°F for 10 to 12 minutes or until edges are lightly browned. Cool on cookie sheets 1 minute. Remove to cooling racks; cool completely.   *Makes 5 dozen cookies*

Favorite recipe from Wisconsin Milk Marketing Board

ORANGE SUGAR COOKIES

2 cups all-purpose flour
1½ teaspoons baking soda
½ cup FLEISCHMANN'S® Margarine, softened
1 cup sugar

2 teaspoons grated orange peel
1 teaspoon vanilla extract
¼ cup EGG BEATERS® 99% Real Egg Product
Additional sugar (optional)

In small bowl, combine flour and baking soda; set aside.

In medium bowl with electric mixer at medium speed, beat margarine, 1 cup sugar, orange peel and vanilla until creamy. Add egg product; beat until smooth. Gradually stir in flour mixture until blended. Cover; chill dough 1 hour.

Shape dough into 42 (¾-inch) balls; roll in additional sugar, if desired. Place on lightly greased baking sheets, about 2 inches apart. Bake at 375°F for 8 to 10 minutes or until light golden brown. Remove from baking sheets; cool on wire racks.   *Makes 3½ dozen cookies*

OATMEAL SCOTCHIES

1¼ cups all-purpose flour
1 teaspoon baking soda
½ teaspoon salt
½ teaspoon cinnamon
1 cup (2 sticks) butter, softened
¾ cup granulated sugar
¾ cup firmly packed brown sugar
2 eggs

1 teaspoon vanilla extract *or* grated
   peel of 1 orange
3 cups quick or old fashioned oats,
   uncooked
2 cups (12-ounce package) NESTLÉ®
   Toll House® Butterscotch
   Flavored Morsels

Preheat oven to 375°F. In small bowl, combine flour, baking soda, salt and cinnamon; set aside.

In large mixer bowl, beat butter, granulated sugar, brown sugar, eggs and vanilla extract until light and fluffy. Gradually beat in flour mixture. Stir in oats and morsels. Drop by measuring tablespoonfuls onto ungreased cookie sheets. Bake 7 to 8 minutes for chewier cookies (9 to 10 minutes for crisper cookies). Remove from cookie sheets; cool completely.   *Makes about 4 dozen cookies*

PEANUT BUTTER COOKIES

⅔ cup firmly packed light brown
   sugar
½ cup chunky or smooth peanut
   butter
⅓ cup BLUE BONNET® Margarine,
   softened

1 egg
½ cup Regular, Instant or Quick
   CREAM OF WHEAT® Cereal
1 teaspoon vanilla extract
1¼ cups all-purpose flour
½ teaspoon baking soda

In medium bowl with electric mixer at medium speed, beat brown sugar, peanut butter, margarine and egg until fluffy; blend in cereal and vanilla. Stir in flour and baking soda to make stiff dough.

Shape dough into 1-inch balls. Place 2 inches apart on greased baking sheets. Flatten balls with bottom of floured glass; press with fork tines to make criss-cross pattern. Bake at 350°F for 8 to 9 minutes or until lightly browned. Remove from baking sheets; cool on wire racks.   *Makes 4 dozen cookies*

Oatmeal Scotchies

PINEAPPLE–OATMEAL COOKIES

1 can (20 ounces) DOLE® Crushed
    Pineapple in Syrup*
1½ cups brown sugar, packed
1 cup margarine
1 egg
3 cups rolled oats, uncooked
2 cups all-purpose flour

1 teaspoon baking powder
1 teaspoon ground cinnamon
½ teaspoon salt
1 cup DOLE® Raisins
1 cup DOLE® Natural Almonds,
    toasted and chopped

• Drain pineapple well. Reserve ½ cup syrup.

• Beat sugar and margarine in large bowl until light and fluffy. Beat in egg, drained pineapple and reserved ½ cup syrup. Combine remaining ingredients in medium bowl; blend into pineapple mixture.

• Drop by 2 heaping tablespoonfuls, 2 inches apart, onto greased cookie sheets. Flatten tops with back of spoon.

• Bake in 350°F oven 20 to 25 minutes or until golden. Cool on wire racks.

Makes about 2½ dozen cookies

*Use pineapple packed in juice, if desired.

AUNTIE VAN'S CHRISTMAS COOKIES

2 cups granulated sugar
1 cup butter, softened
2 eggs
1 teaspoon vanilla
5 cups all-purpose flour

1 teaspoon baking soda
1 cup sour cream
    Coffee Frosting (page 125) or
    canned vanilla frosting

Beat granulated sugar and 1 cup butter in large bowl until light and fluffy. Blend in eggs and 1 teaspoon vanilla. Combine flour and baking soda; add alternately with sour cream, mixing well after each addition. Refrigerate 6 hours or overnight. Divide dough into 4 pieces. Roll out 1 piece on lightly floured surface to ⅛-inch thickness (keep remaining dough refrigerated). Cut into desired shapes; place on ungreased cookie sheets. Bake at 325°F for 10 to 12 minutes or until bottoms are golden brown. Repeat with remaining dough. Cool completely. Frost with Coffee Frosting.

Makes 6 dozen cookies

COFFEE FROSTING

1 tablespoon instant coffee granules
1 tablespoon hot water
6 tablespoons butter, softened

1 teaspoon vanilla
3 cups sifted powdered sugar
¼ to ⅓ cup whipping cream

Dissolve coffee granules in water. Beat 6 tablespoons butter in medium bowl until fluffy. Stir in coffee mixture and 1 teaspoon vanilla. Add powdered sugar; mix until well combined. Gradually add whipping cream until of good spreading consistency.

Favorite recipe from Wisconsin Milk Marketing Board

SESAME–ALMOND COOKIES

1 cup FILIPPO BERIO® Brand Olive
   Oil
1 (2-inch) strip lemon peel
4 teaspoons sesame seeds
½ cup dry white wine
1 teaspoon grated lemon peel

1 teaspoon grated orange peel
⅓ cup sugar
½ cup sliced almonds
3½ cups all-purpose flour
1 tablespoon ground cinnamon

1. Heat oil, 2-inch strip lemon peel and sesame seeds in large skillet over medium heat until seeds are lightly browned. Remove from heat; cool.

2. Remove lemon peel strip. Pour oil and sesame seeds into large bowl. Add wine, grated lemon and orange peels, sugar and almonds; stir.

3. Combine flour and cinnamon in small bowl. Add to oil mixture gradually, stirring well. Gather dough into ball; knead once or twice until smooth. Set aside to rest for 30 minutes.

4. Preheat oven to 350°F. Divide dough into 18 equal pieces. Roll each into a ball and flatten to about 3 inches across and ¼ inch thick. Place on lightly greased baking sheet. Bake 20 minutes or until lightly browned and firm. Cool on wire rack. Store in covered container.   *Makes 18 cookies*

PEANUT BUTTER PIZZA COOKIES

COOKIES

1¼ cups firmly packed light brown
   sugar
¾ cup creamy peanut butter
½ cup CRISCO® All-Vegetable
   Shortening
3 tablespoons milk

1 tablespoon vanilla
1 egg
1¾ cups all-purpose flour
¾ teaspoon salt
¾ teaspoon baking soda

PIZZA SAUCE

1 cup (6-ounce package) milk
   chocolate chips

2 tablespoons CRISCO® All-Vegetable
   Shortening

PIZZA TOPPING

An assortment of the following:
   candy coated chocolate pieces,
   miniature marshmallows,

assorted nuts, raisins, gummy
   bears, gumdrops, etc.

DRIZZLE

½ cup white chocolate chips
½ teaspoon CRISCO® All-Vegetable
   Shortening

1. Heat oven to 350°F. Place foil on 2 baking sheets. Trace 7-inch circle on foil using pan lid. Grease foil.

2. **For cookies,** combine brown sugar, peanut butter, shortening, milk and vanilla in large bowl. Beat at medium speed of electric mixer until well blended. Add egg. Beat until just blended. Combine flour, salt and baking soda in small bowl. Add to brown sugar mixture at low speed. Mix until just blended. Divide dough into 4 equal portions. Shape each into disk. Place disk in middle of circle and spread evenly to edge with hands.

3. Bake 15 to 16 minutes or until set. Use back of spoon to flatten center and up to edge of each hot cookie to resemble pizza crust. Cool 5 to 8 minutes on baking sheet. Remove cookie on foil to cool completely.

4. **For pizza sauce,** combine milk chocolate chips and shortening in large microwave-safe measuring cup or bowl. Microwave at MEDIUM (50% power) for 2 to 4 minutes or until chips are shiny and soft. (Or, melt on rangetop in small saucepan on very low heat.) Stir until smooth. Spoon ¼ of chocolate mixture into center of each pizza cookie. Spread to edge of depressed area. Sprinkle desired toppings over chocolate.

5. **For drizzle,** place white chocolate chips and shortening in heavy resealable plastic food storage bag. Seal. Microwave at MEDIUM (50% power). Knead bag after 1 minute. Repeat until smooth (or melt by placing in bowl of hot water). Cut pinpoint hole in corner of bag. Drizzle over cookies.

Makes 4 large pizza cookies

Peanut Butter Pizza Cookies

Top to bottom: Mini Morsel Granola Cookies; Banana Bars (page 137)

MINI MORSEL GRANOLA COOKIES

2½ cups all-purpose flour
2 teaspoons baking powder
1 teaspoon baking soda
1 teaspoon cinnamon
1 cup (2 sticks) butter, softened
1¼ cups firmly packed brown sugar

2 eggs
2 cups (12-ounce package) NESTLÉ®
   Toll House® Semi-Sweet
   Chocolate Mini Morsels
2 cups granola cereal
1 cup raisins

Preheat oven to 375°F. In small bowl, combine flour, baking powder, baking soda and cinnamon; set aside.

In large mixer bowl, beat butter and brown sugar until light and fluffy. Beat in eggs. Gradually beat in flour mixture. Stir in morsels, granola and raisins. Drop by rounded measuring tablespoonfuls onto ungreased cookie sheets. Bake 9 to 11 minutes until edges are golden brown. Let stand on cookie sheets 5 minutes. Remove from cookie sheets; cool.
Makes about 4 dozen cookies

NORWEGIAN MOLASSES COOKIES

2¼ cups all-purpose flour
2 teaspoons baking soda
1 cup firmly packed light brown
   sugar
¾ cup FLEISCHMANN'S® Margarine,
   softened
¼ cup EGG BEATERS® 99% Real Egg
   Product

¼ cup BRER RABBIT® Light or Dark
   Molasses
¼ cup granulated sugar
   Water
   Confectioners' Sugar Glaze (recipe
   follows) (optional)
   Colored sprinkles (optional)

In small bowl, combine flour and baking soda; set aside.

In medium bowl with electric mixer at medium speed, beat brown sugar and margarine. Add egg product and molasses; beat until smooth. Stir in flour mixture. Cover; chill dough 1 hour.

Shape dough into 48 (1¼-inch) balls; roll in granulated sugar. Place on greased and floured baking sheets, about 2 inches apart. Lightly sprinkle dough with water. Bake at 350°F for 18 to 20 minutes or until flattened. Remove from sheets; cool on wire racks. Prepare Confectioners' Sugar Glaze. Decorate with glaze and colored sprinkles, if desired.   *Makes 4 dozen cookies*

Confectioners' Sugar Glaze: Combine 1 cup confectioners' sugar and 5 to 6 teaspoons skim milk.

GIANT OATMEAL COOKIES

1 cup firmly packed brown sugar
¾ cup (1½ sticks) margarine or
   butter, softened
2 eggs
1 teaspoon vanilla
1¼ cups all-purpose flour
½ teaspoon baking soda

½ teaspoon salt (optional)
2½ cups QUAKER® Oats (Quick or Old
   Fashioned), uncooked
One 6-ounce package (1 cup)
   semisweet chocolate pieces
½ cup chopped nuts

Heat oven to 350°F. Lightly grease 2 large cookie sheets. Beat sugar and margarine until light and fluffy. Blend in eggs and vanilla. Add combined flour, baking soda, salt and oats; mix well. Stir in chocolate pieces and nuts. Divide dough in half. Press each half into circle about ¾ inch thick on prepared cookie sheets. Bake 17 to 20 minutes or until lightly browned. Cool 5 minutes on cookie sheets; remove to wire racks. Cool completely. Cut into wedges to serve.   *Makes 2 giant cookies*

Variation: Drop dough by rounded tablespoonfuls onto greased cookie sheets. Bake 10 to 12 minutes. Makes about 3 dozen cookies.

Marvelous Macaroons

MARVELOUS MACAROONS

1 can (8 ounces) DOLE® Crushed
    Pineapple in Juice
1 can (14 ounces) sweetened
    condensed milk
1 package (7 ounces) flaked coconut
½ cup DOLE® Chopped Almonds,
    toasted

½ cup margarine, melted
    Grated peel from 1 DOLE® Lemon
¼ teaspoon almond extract
1 cup all-purpose flour
1 teaspoon baking powder

- Drain pineapple well. Reserve juice for beverage.

- Combine drained pineapple, sweetened condensed milk, coconut, almonds, margarine, 1 teaspoon lemon peel and almond extract in large bowl; mix well.

- Combine flour and baking powder in small bowl. Beat into pineapple mixture until blended.

- Drop by heaping tablespoonfuls, 1 inch apart, onto greased cookie sheets.

- Bake in 350°F oven 13 to 15 minutes. Cool on wire racks. Store in refrigerator.

Makes 3½ dozen cookies

FAVORITE PEANUT BUTTER COOKIES

½ cup peanut butter
¼ cup (½ stick) margarine or butter,
    softened
¾ cup sugar
1 egg, beaten

½ cup all-purpose flour
½ teaspoon baking powder
¼ teaspoon salt (optional)
2 cups Rice CHEX® brand cereal,
    crushed to 1 cup

Preheat oven to 350°F. Lightly grease cookie sheet. In large bowl, beat peanut butter, margarine and sugar. Add egg. Stir in flour and baking powder; add salt, if desired. Stir in cereal; mix well. For each cookie, roll 1 level tablespoon dough into ball. Place on prepared cookie sheet. With fork dipped in sugar, flatten slightly in criss-cross pattern. Bake 8 to 10 minutes or until bottoms are lightly browned. Let stand 1 minute before removing from cookie sheet. Cool on wire rack. *Makes 2½ dozen cookies*

Brownies & Bars

Rich brownies and delicious bar cookies are quick to make and will satisfy the cookie monster in your house.

ONE BOWL BROWNIES

4 squares BAKER'S® Unsweetened
    Chocolate
¾ cup (1½ sticks) margarine or
    butter
2 cups sugar

3 eggs
1 teaspoon vanilla
1 cup all-purpose flour
1 cup chopped nuts (optional)

Heat oven to 350°F. Microwave chocolate and margarine in large microwavable bowl on HIGH (100% power) 2 minutes or until margarine is melted. Stir until chocolate is completely melted. Stir sugar into melted chocolate mixture. Mix in eggs and vanilla until well blended. Stir in flour and nuts. Spread in greased 13×9-inch pan.

Bake 30 to 35 minutes or until toothpick inserted into center comes out with fudgy crumbs. *Do not overbake.* Cool in pan; cut into bars.

Makes about 24 brownies

Prep time: 10 minutes
Baking time: 30 to 35 minutes

Tips:

• For cakelike brownies, stir in ½ cup milk with eggs and vanilla. Increase flour to 1½ cups.

• When using a glass baking dish, reduce oven temperature to 325°F.

Top to bottom: Peanut Butter Swirl Brownies (page 134); Rocky Road Brownies (page 134)

Rocky Road Brownies: Prepare One Bowl Brownie batter as directed. Bake at 350°F for 30 minutes. Sprinkle 2 cups KRAFT® Miniature Marshmallows, 1 cup BAKER'S® Semi-Sweet Real Chocolate Chips and 1 cup chopped nuts over brownies immediately. Continue baking 3 to 5 minutes or until topping begins to melt together. Cool in pan; cut into bars. Makes about 24 brownies.

Prep time: 15 minutes
Baking time: 35 minutes

Peanut Butter Swirl Brownies: Prepare One Bowl Brownie batter as directed, reserving 1 tablespoon margarine and 2 tablespoons sugar. Spread batter in greased 13×9-inch pan. Add reserved ingredients to ⅔ cup peanut butter; mix well. Place teaspoonfuls of peanut butter mixture over brownie batter. Swirl with knife to marbleize. Bake at 350°F for 30 to 35 minutes or until toothpick inserted into center comes out with fudgy crumbs. Cool in pan; cut into bars. Makes about 24 brownies.

Prep time: 15 minutes
Baking time: 30 to 35 minutes

PECAN TURTLE BARS

1½ cups all-purpose flour	1 cup pecan halves
1½ cups packed brown sugar, divided	⅔ cup butter
½ cup butter, softened	1 cup milk chocolate pieces

Combine flour, 1 cup brown sugar and ½ cup softened butter in large mixer bowl. Beat at medium speed of electric mixer 2 to 3 minutes or until mixture resembles fine crumbs. Pat mixture evenly onto bottom of ungreased 13×9-inch baking pan. Sprinkle pecans evenly over crumb mixture.

Combine ⅔ cup butter and remaining ½ cup brown sugar in small saucepan. Cook and stir over medium heat until entire surface is bubbly. Cook and stir one half to 1 minute more. Pour into pan, spreading evenly over crust. Bake in 350°F oven 18 to 20 minutes or until entire surface is bubbly. Remove from oven; immediately sprinkle with chocolate pieces. Let stand 2 to 3 minutes to allow chocolate to melt; use knife to swirl chocolate slightly. Cool completely in pan on wire rack. Use sharp knife to cut into 48 bars.

Makes 48 bars

Favorite recipe from Wisconsin Milk Marketing Board

BLACK RUSSIAN BROWNIES

4 squares (1 ounce *each*)
  unsweetened chocolate
1 cup butter
¾ teaspoon ground black pepper
4 eggs, lightly beaten
1½ cups sugar
1½ teaspoons vanilla
⅓ cup KAHLÚA®

2 tablespoons vodka
1⅓ cups all-purpose flour
½ teaspoon salt
¼ teaspoon baking powder
1 cup chopped walnuts or toasted
  sliced almonds
Powdered sugar (optional)

Line bottom of 13×9-inch baking pan with waxed paper. Melt chocolate and butter with black pepper in small saucepan over low heat. Remove from heat.

Combine eggs, sugar and vanilla in large bowl; beat well. Stir in cooled chocolate mixture, Kahlúa® and vodka. Combine flour, salt and baking powder; add to chocolate mixture and stir until blended. Add walnuts. Spread in prepared pan.

Bake in 350°F oven just until toothpick inserted into center comes out clean, about 25 minutes. *Do not overbake.* Cool in pan on wire rack. Cut into bars. Sprinkle with powdered sugar, if desired.

Makes about 30 brownies

BAKED S'MORES

1 package DUNCAN HINES® Golden
  Sugar Cookie Mix
1 egg
1 tablespoon water

3 bars (1.55 ounces each) milk
  chocolate
1 jar (7 ounces) marshmallow creme

1. Preheat oven to 350°F. Grease 8-inch square pan.

2. Combine cookie mix, contents of buttery flavor packet from Mix, egg and water in large bowl. Stir until thoroughly blended. Divide cookie dough in half. Press half the dough evenly into bottom of pan.

3. Cut each milk chocolate bar into 12 sections following division marks on bars. Arrange chocolate sections into 4 rows, with 9 sections in each row, on top of dough.

4. Place spoonfuls of marshmallow creme on top of chocolate. Spread to cover chocolate and cookie dough. Drop remaining cookie dough by teaspoonfuls on top of marshmallow creme. Spread slightly with back of spoon. Bake at 350°F for 25 to 30 minutes or until light golden brown. Cool completely. Cut into squares.

Makes 9 squares

FRUIT AND CHOCOLATE DREAM SQUARES

TOPPING
⅔ **cup all-purpose flour**
½ **cup pecans, chopped**
⅓ **cup firmly packed brown sugar**

6 **tablespoons (¾ stick) butter,
softened**

CRUST
1¼ **cups all-purpose flour**
½ **cup granulated sugar**
½ **cup (1 stick) butter**
½ **cup strawberry or raspberry jam**

2 **cups (11.5-ounce package) NESTLÉ®
Toll House® Milk Chocolate
Morsels**

Topping: In small bowl, combine ⅔ cup flour, pecans and brown sugar. With pastry blender or 2 knives, cut in 6 tablespoons butter until mixture resembles coarse crumbs; set aside.

Crust: Preheat oven to 375°F. Grease 9-inch square baking pan. In small bowl, combine 1¼ cups flour and granulated sugar. With pastry blender or 2 knives, cut in ½ cup butter until mixture resembles fine crumbs. Press into prepared pan.

Bake 20 to 25 minutes or until set but not brown. Spread with jam. Top with morsels and Topping.

Bake 15 to 20 minutes longer or until top is lightly browned. Cool completely; cut into 2¼-inch squares.
Makes 16 squares

PEANUT BUTTER RAISIN BARS

¼ **cup firmly packed light brown
sugar**
¼ **cup corn syrup**
¼ **cup chunky peanut butter**

2 **cups SPOON SIZE® Shredded
Wheat, coarsely crushed**
¾ **cup seedless raisins**

In large saucepan over medium heat, stir together brown sugar and corn syrup until sugar dissolves and mixture is warm. Remove from heat; blend in peanut butter. Stir in cereal and raisins until well coated. Press into lightly greased 8×8-inch baking pan. Cool until firm. Cut into 24 bars. Store in airtight container.
Makes 24 bars

Fruit and Chocolate Dream Squares

BANANA BARS

1½ cups all-purpose flour
½ cup whole wheat flour
2 teaspoons baking powder
½ teaspoon salt
¾ cup (1½ sticks) butter, softened
⅔ cup granulated sugar
⅔ cup firmly packed light brown
   sugar

1 teaspoon vanilla extract
2 medium bananas, mashed
1 egg
2 cups (12-ounce package) NESTLÉ®
   Toll House® Semi-Sweet
   Chocolate Mini Morsels
Confectioners' sugar

Preheat oven to 350°F. In small bowl, combine flours, baking powder and salt; set aside.

In large mixer bowl, beat butter, granulated sugar, brown sugar and vanilla extract until light and fluffy. Beat in bananas and egg. Gradually beat in flour mixture. Stir in morsels. Spread into greased 15½×10½-inch baking pan.

Bake 25 to 30 minutes. Cool completely. Sprinkle with confectioners' sugar. Cut into 2×1-inch bars.

Makes about 6½ dozen bars

Pineapple Pecan Bars

PINEAPPLE PECAN BARS

CRUST
  2 cups all-purpose flour
  ⅔ cup powdered sugar

1 cup margarine

PINEAPPLE TOPPING
  1 can (20 ounces) DOLE® Crushed
    Pineapple in Syrup or Juice,
    drained
  4 eggs

¾ cup brown sugar, packed
⅓ cup all-purpose flour
2 cups coarsely chopped pecans

For crust, combine 2 cups flour and powdered sugar. Cut in margarine until mixture is crumbly. Press into bottom of 13×9-inch baking pan. Bake in 350°F oven 15 minutes. Remove from oven.

For topping, combine drained pineapple, eggs, brown sugar and ⅓ cup flour. Stir in pecans. Pour over partially baked crust. Bake in 350°F oven 30 to 35 minutes or until set. Cool completely. Cut into bars.

Makes 32 bars

RASPBERRY MERINGUE BARS

1 cup butter or margarine, softened
½ cup firmly packed brown sugar
1 egg

2 cups all-purpose flour
1 can SOLO® *or* 1 jar BAKER®
  Raspberry Filling

MERINGUE TOPPING
  3 egg whites
  ¾ cup granulated sugar

½ cup shredded coconut
½ cup slivered almonds

Preheat oven to 325°F. Grease 13×9-inch baking pan. Beat butter and brown sugar in medium bowl with electric mixer at medium speed until light and fluffy. Add 1 egg; beat until blended. Stir in flour until well combined. Pat dough evenly in prepared pan. Bake 20 minutes. Remove from oven; spread raspberry filling over crust. (Do not turn oven off.)

For Meringue Topping, beat egg whites in medium bowl with electric mixer at high speed until soft peaks form. Add granulated sugar gradually; beat until stiff and glossy. Fold coconut and almonds into beaten egg white mixture. Spread over raspberry filling. Return to oven. Bake 20 minutes or until Meringue Topping is lightly browned. Cool completely in pan on wire rack. Cut into 48 bars.

Makes 48 bars

Chocolate Apple Crisp

CHOCOLATE APPLE CRISP

1½ cups all-purpose flour
1 cup firmly packed brown sugar
½ teaspoon baking soda
¼ teaspoon salt
¾ cup (1½ sticks) butter
1½ cups quick oats, uncooked

2 cups (12-ounce package) NESTLÉ®
   Toll House® Semi-Sweet
   Chocolate Mini Morsels
3 apples, unpeeled if desired,
   chopped
1 cup pecans or walnuts, chopped

Preheat oven to 375°F. In large bowl, combine flour, brown sugar, baking soda and salt. With pastry blender or 2 knives, cut in butter until mixture resembles fine crumbs. Stir in oats; press half of oat mixture into greased 13×9-inch baking pan.

To remaining oat mixture, add morsels, apples and pecans; stir to combine. Sprinkle over base.

Bake 35 to 40 minutes or until lightly browned. Cool slightly; cut into squares.

Makes about 15 servings

MOCHA BROWNIES

1¼ cups all-purpose flour
1 teaspoon baking powder
½ teaspoon salt
4 (1-ounce) squares semisweet
    chocolate
¾ cup BLUE BONNET® Margarine
1 tablespoon instant coffee granules

1 cup granulated sugar
4 eggs
1 teaspoon vanilla extract
1¼ cups PLANTERS® Walnuts, chopped
    and divided
Creamy Coffee Frosting (recipe
    follows)

In small bowl, combine flour, baking powder and salt; set aside.

In large saucepan over low heat, stir together chocolate, margarine and 1 tablespoon coffee granules until blended. Remove from heat; stir in granulated sugar. Add eggs, 1 at a time, beating well after each addition. Stir in flour mixture and vanilla until blended. Stir in 1 cup walnuts. Spread in greased 13×9-inch baking pan.

Bake at 350°F for 25 to 30 minutes. Cool in pan on wire rack. Prepare Creamy Coffee Frosting; spread on brownies. Sprinkle with remaining ¼ cup walnuts. Cut into 2×1½-inch bars.   *Makes about 32 bars*

Creamy Coffee Frosting: Dissolve 1 teaspoon instant coffee granules in ¼ cup milk. In small bowl with electric mixer at high speed, beat 4 ounces cream cheese and milk mixture until creamy. Gradually beat in 1 (16-ounce) package confectioners' sugar until well blended and good spreading consistency.

FROSTED TOFFEE BARS

2 cups QUAKER® Oats (Quick or Old
    Fashioned), uncooked
½ cup firmly packed brown sugar
½ cup (1 stick) margarine or butter,
    melted

½ cup semisweet chocolate pieces
¼ cup chopped peanuts

Heat oven to 350°F. Lightly grease 9-inch square baking pan. In large bowl, combine oats, brown sugar and margarine; mix well. Spread into prepared pan. Bake 13 minutes or until light golden brown; cool on wire rack.

In small saucepan over low heat, melt chocolate pieces. Spread over baked oat mixture; sprinkle with peanuts. Chill 4 hours or until chocolate is set. Cut into 2×1½-inch bars. Store tightly covered in refrigerator.   *Makes about 28 bars*

RICH 'N' CREAMY BROWNIE BARS

BROWNIES
1 package DUNCAN HINES®
    Chocolate Lovers' Double Fudge
    Brownie Mix
2 eggs

⅓ cup water
¼ cup CRISCO® Oil or CRISCO®
    PURITAN® Oil
½ cup chopped pecans

TOPPING
1 package (8 ounces) cream cheese,
    softened
2 eggs

1 pound (3½ cups) confectioners'
    sugar
1 teaspoon vanilla extract

1. Preheat oven to 350°F. Grease bottom of 13×9-inch pan.

2. **For brownies,** combine brownie mix, contents of fudge packet from Mix, 2 eggs, water and oil in large bowl. Stir with spoon until well blended, about 50 strokes. Stir in pecans. Spread evenly in pan.

3. **For topping,** beat cream cheese in large bowl at medium speed with electric mixer until smooth. Beat in 2 eggs, confectioners' sugar and vanilla extract until smooth. Spread evenly over brownie mixture. Bake at 350°F for 45 to 50 minutes or until edges and top are golden brown and shiny. Cool completely. Refrigerate until well chilled. Cut into bars.   *Makes 48 bars*

SPICED MINCEMEAT SQUARES

½ cup all-purpose flour
½ teaspoon ground cinnamon
¼ teaspoon ground nutmeg
¼ teaspoon baking soda
⅓ cup BLUE BONNET® Margarine,
    softened
½ cup firmly packed light brown
    sugar

1 egg
1 cup prepared mincemeat
1 cup NABISCO® 100% Bran
    Confectioners' Sugar Glaze
    (page 129)

In small bowl, combine flour, cinnamon, nutmeg and baking soda; set aside.

In medium bowl with electric mixer at medium speed, beat margarine and brown sugar until light and fluffy. Beat in egg. Add flour mixture, mincemeat and bran. Spread into greased 9×9-inch baking pan. Bake at 400°F for 20 to 25 minutes or until knife inserted into center comes out clean. Cool on wire rack. Drizzle with Confectioners' Sugar Glaze. Cut into 2¼-inch squares. Store in airtight container.   *Makes 16 squares*

Rich 'n' Creamy Brownie Bars

Banana Gingerbread Bars

BANANA GINGERBREAD BARS

1 extra-ripe, medium DOLE® Banana,
   peeled
1 package (14.5 ounces) gingerbread
   cake mix
½ cup lukewarm water
1 egg
1 small DOLE® Banana, peeled and
   chopped (½ cup)

½ cup DOLE® Raisins
½ cup DOLE® Slivered Almonds
1½ cups powdered sugar
   Juice from 1 DOLE® Lemon

• Place medium banana in blender. Process until puréed; use ½ cup for recipe.

• Combine gingerbread cake mix, water, ½ cup puréed banana and egg in large bowl. Beat well.

• Stir in chopped banana, raisins and almonds.

• Spread batter in greased 13×9-inch baking pan. Bake in 350°F oven 20 to 25 minutes or until toothpick inserted in center comes out clean.

• Mix powdered sugar and 3 tablespoons lemon juice in medium bowl to make thin glaze. Spread over warm gingerbread. Cool. Cut into bars. Sprinkle with additional powdered sugar, if desired.

Makes 32 bars

OATMEAL EXTRAVAGANZAS

1 cup all-purpose flour	**1 egg**
1½ teaspoons baking powder	**2 tablespoons water**
½ teaspoon salt	**2 cups quick oats, uncooked**
1 cup firmly packed brown sugar	**2 cups (12-ounce package) NESTLÉ®**
¾ cup (1½ sticks) butter, softened	**Toll House® Semi-Sweet**
1 teaspoon vanilla extract	**Chocolate Morsels**

Preheat oven to 375°F. In small bowl, combine flour, baking powder and salt; set aside.

In large mixer bowl, beat brown sugar, butter and vanilla extract until light and fluffy. Beat in egg. Gradually blend in flour mixture, then water. Stir in oats and morsels. Spread in greased 9-inch square pan.

Bake 30 to 35 minutes. Cool; cut into 1½-inch squares.   *Makes 3 dozen squares*

MALLOW–GRAHAM BARS

2 tablespoons BLUE BONNET®	**½ cup seedless raisins**
Margarine	**½ cup chopped dry roasted peanuts**
3 cups miniature marshmallows	
1 stay fresh package HONEY MAID®	
Honey Grahams, coarsely	
chopped	

In large saucepan over low heat, melt margarine. Add marshmallows; stir until melted. Remove from heat; stir in graham crackers, raisins and peanuts. Spread mixture into greased 9×9-inch baking pan. Cool 1 hour or until firm. Cut into 18 bars. Store in airtight container.   *Makes 18 bars*

Fanciful Cookies

Beautiful to look at and great-tasting, these cookies take a little extra time to prepare—but they're worth it!

CHOCOLATE–GILDED DANISH SUGAR CONES

½ cup butter or margarine, softened
½ cup sugar
½ cup all-purpose flour
2 egg whites

1 teaspoon vanilla
3 ounces bittersweet chocolate *or*
 ½ cup semisweet chocolate chips

Preheat oven to 400°F. Generously grease 4 cookie sheets. Beat butter and sugar in large bowl until light and fluffy. Blend in flour. In clean, dry bowl, beat egg whites until frothy. Blend into butter mixture; add vanilla.

Using measuring teaspoon, place 4 mounds of dough, 4 inches apart, on each prepared cookie sheet. Spread mounds with back of spoon dipped in water to 3-inch diameter. Bake, 1 sheet at a time, 5 to 6 minutes or until edges are just barely golden. (Do not overbake or cookies become crisp too quickly and are difficult to shape.) Remove from oven and quickly loosen each cookie from cookie sheet with thin spatula. Shape each into a cone; cones become firm as they cool. (If cookies become too firm to shape, return to oven for a few seconds to soften.)

Melt chocolate in small bowl over hot, not boiling, water. Stir until smooth. When all cookies are baked and cooled, dip flared ends into melted chocolate. Let stand until chocolate is set. If desired, serve cones by standing them in a bowl. (Adding about 1 inch of sugar to bottom of bowl may be necessary to hold them upright.)

Makes 16 cookies

Chocolate-Gilded Danish Sugar Cones

SNOW CAPS

3 egg whites
¼ teaspoon cream of tartar
¾ cup sugar
½ teaspoon vanilla extract

1 cup (6 ounces) semisweet
  chocolate chips
2 white chocolate baking bars
  (2 ounces each), chopped
  (optional)

Preheat oven to 200°F. Line baking sheets with parchment paper. In large mixer bowl, combine egg whites and cream of tartar. Beat at highest speed of electric mixer until mixture is just frothy. Add sugar, 1 tablespoon at a time, beating well after each addition. Beat until stiff peaks form. Add vanilla; beat 1 minute. Fold in chocolate chips. Drop mixture by teaspoonfuls, 1 inch apart, onto prepared baking sheets. Bake 2 hours or until meringues are thoroughly dry to touch but not browned, rotating baking sheets halfway through baking. Turn off heat. Leave in closed oven 3 to 4 hours or until completely dry. Remove from oven. Cool completely. Carefully remove from parchment.

Melt white chocolate in top of double boiler over hot, not boiling, water. Stir constantly until chocolate melts. Dip top of each cookie into melted chocolate, if desired. Place on waxed paper to dry. Store at room temperature in tightly covered containers.   *Makes about 6 dozen cookies*

Orange Pecan Gems

ORANGE PECAN GEMS

1 package DUNCAN HINES® Moist
    Deluxe Orange Supreme Cake Mix
1 container (8 ounces) vanilla low
    fat yogurt
1 egg

2 tablespoons butter or margarine,
    softened
1 cup finely chopped pecans
1 cup pecan halves

1. Preheat oven to 350°F. Grease baking sheets.

2. Combine cake mix, yogurt, egg, butter and chopped pecans in large bowl. Beat at low speed with electric mixer until blended. Drop by rounded teaspoonfuls 2 inches apart onto greased baking sheets. Press pecan half onto center of each cookie. Bake at 350°F for 11 to 13 minutes or until golden brown. Cool 1 minute on baking sheets. Remove to cooling racks. Cool completely. Store in airtight container.

Makes 4½ to 5 dozen cookies

Tip: Cookies may be stored in airtight container in freezer for up to 6 months.

OATMEAL CRANBERRY–NUT COOKIES

1¼ cups firmly packed light brown
    sugar
¾ cup BUTTER FLAVOR* CRISCO®
    All-Vegetable Shortening
1 egg
⅓ cup milk
1½ teaspoons vanilla
3 cups quick oats, uncooked

1 cup all-purpose flour
1¼ teaspoons cinnamon
½ teaspoon baking soda
½ teaspoon salt
¼ teaspoon allspice
1 cup crushed whole-berry
    cranberry sauce
½ cup sliced almonds, broken

1. Heat oven to 375°F. Grease baking sheets.

2. Combine brown sugar, shortening, egg, milk and vanilla in large bowl. Beat at medium speed of electric mixer until well blended.

3. Combine oats, flour, cinnamon, baking soda, salt and allspice in small bowl. Mix into brown sugar mixture at low speed just until blended. Stir in cranberry sauce and almonds.

4. Drop rounded tablespoonfuls of dough 2 inches apart onto prepared baking sheets.

5. Bake at 375°F for 10 to 12 minutes or until lightly browned. Cool 2 minutes on baking sheets. Remove to wire racks to cool completely.

Makes about 4 dozen cookies

*BUTTER FLAVOR CRISCO® is artificially flavored.

CHERRY SURPRISES

COOKIES
⅔ cup granulated sugar
½ cup BUTTER FLAVOR* CRISCO®
   All-Vegetable Shortening
1 egg
2 tablespoons light corn syrup or
   regular pancake syrup

1 teaspoon vanilla
1¾ cups all-purpose flour
½ teaspoon baking powder
¼ teaspoon baking soda
¼ teaspoon salt
48 candied cherries

DRIZZLE
½ cup semi-sweet chocolate chips
1 teaspoon BUTTER FLAVOR*
   CRISCO® All-Vegetable
   Shortening

1. Heat oven to 375°F.

2. **For cookies,** combine sugar and ½ cup shortening in large bowl. Beat at medium speed of electric mixer until well blended. Add egg, corn syrup and vanilla. Beat until light and fluffy.

3. Combine flour, baking powder, baking soda and salt. Add gradually to sugar mixture at low speed. Mix until well blended. Divide dough into 48 equal pieces.

4. Shape thin layer of dough around each cherry. Place 2 inches apart on ungreased baking sheets.

5. Bake at 375°F for 8 minutes or until set but not browned. Cool 2 minutes on baking sheets. Remove to wire racks to cool completely.

6. **For drizzle,** place chocolate chips and 1 teaspoon shortening in heavy resealable sandwich bag. Seal. Microwave at MEDIUM (50% power). Knead bag after 1 minute. Repeat until smooth (or melt by placing in bowl of hot water). Cut pinpoint hole in corner of bag. Squeeze out melted chocolate; drizzle over cookies. Allow drizzle to set before storing between layers of waxed paper in airtight container.

Makes 4 dozen cookies

Tip: Well-drained maraschino cherries may be substituted for candied cherries.

*BUTTER FLAVOR CRISCO® is artificially flavored.

Cherry Surprises

FLORENTINE CUPS

BASE
2 cups HONEY ALMOND DELIGHT®
   brand cereal, crushed to 1 cup
1 cup flaked coconut
½ cup raisins
½ cup all-purpose flour
1½ teaspoons grated fresh orange peel

½ teaspoon baking powder
½ teaspoon ground cinnamon
½ cup packed brown sugar
⅓ cup butter or margarine
¼ cup honey

ICING
1 tablespoon butter or margarine,
   softened
½ cup powdered sugar

1½ teaspoons orange juice
Sliced almonds

To prepare base, preheat oven to 350°F. Grease 32 miniature (1¾-inch) muffin cups. In large bowl, combine cereal, coconut, raisins, flour, orange peel, baking powder and cinnamon; mix well and set aside. In small saucepan, combine brown sugar, ⅓ cup butter and honey. Stir over medium heat until butter is melted and brown sugar is dissolved. Pour over cereal mixture; blend well. Place 1 tablespoon mixture in each prepared muffin cup; press firmly. Bake 8 to 10 minutes or until golden brown (cups will be soft). Cool in pan 15 minutes. Loosen edges. Invert onto wire racks. Cool completely.

To prepare icing, in small bowl, beat 1 tablespoon butter, powdered sugar and orange juice until smooth. With pastry tube, pipe a decorative swirl on top of each cup. Garnish with sliced almonds.

Makes 32 cups

GINGERBREAD COOKIES

½ cup vegetable shortening
⅓ cup packed light brown sugar
¼ cup dark molasses
1 egg white
½ teaspoon vanilla
1½ cups all-purpose flour

½ teaspoon baking soda
¼ teaspoon baking powder
½ teaspoon salt
1 teaspoon ground cinnamon
½ teaspoon ground ginger

Beat shortening, brown sugar, molasses, egg white and vanilla in large bowl at high speed of electric mixer until smooth. Combine flour, baking soda, baking powder, salt and spices in small bowl. Add to shortening mixture; mix well. Cover; refrigerate until firm, about 8 hours or overnight.

Preheat oven to 350°F. Grease cookie sheets. Roll out dough on lightly floured surface to ⅛-inch thickness. Cut into desired shapes with cookie cutters. Place on prepared cookie sheets.

Bake 6 to 8 minutes or until edges begin to brown. Remove to wire racks; cool completely. Decorate as desired.

Makes about 2½ dozen cookies

MOCHA MINT CRISPS

1 cup butter or margarine, softened
1 cup granulated sugar
1 egg
¼ cup light corn syrup
¼ teaspoon peppermint extract
1 teaspoon powdered instant coffee

1 teaspoon hot water
2 cups all-purpose flour
6 tablespoons HERSHEY'S Cocoa
2 teaspoons baking soda
¼ teaspoon salt
Mocha Mint Sugar (recipe follows)

Heat oven to 350°F. In large mixer bowl, beat butter and granulated sugar until light and fluffy. Add egg, corn syrup and peppermint extract; mix thoroughly. Dissolve 1 teaspoon instant coffee in water; stir into butter mixture. Stir together flour, cocoa, baking soda and salt; gradually add to butter mixture, blending thoroughly.

Shape dough into 1-inch balls. (Dough may be refrigerated for a short time for easier handling.) Prepare Mocha Mint Sugar. Roll dough balls in sugar mixture. Place on ungreased cookie sheets, about 2 inches apart. Bake 8 to 10 minutes or until no imprint remains when touched lightly. Cool slightly. Remove from cookie sheets to wire racks. Cool completely. *Makes about 4 dozen cookies*

Mocha Mint Sugar: In small bowl, stir together ¼ cup powdered sugar, 2 tablespoons crushed hard peppermint candies (about 6 candies) and 1½ teaspoons powdered instant coffee.

HOLIDAY TEATIME TREATS

2 packages (3 ounces each) cream
   cheese, softened
1 cup butter or margarine, softened

2 tablespoons sugar
2 cups all-purpose flour

FILLING
½ cup sugar
2 eggs
¼ cup all-purpose flour
1 teaspoon vanilla

1 can SOLO® *or* 1 jar BAKER® Apricot
   or other fruit filling
½ cup chopped nuts (optional)

Preheat oven to 350°F. Beat cream cheese, butter and 2 tablespoons sugar in medium bowl with electric mixer until fluffy. Stir in 2 cups flour to make soft dough. Divide dough in half. Shape each piece of dough into about 24 (1-inch) balls. Press balls into bottom and up side of ungreased miniature (1¾-inch) muffin cups. Set aside.

To make filling, beat ½ cup sugar, eggs, ¼ cup flour, vanilla and apricot filling in medium bowl with electric mixer until blended. Stir in nuts. Spoon evenly into pastry-lined muffin cups. Bake 25 to 30 minutes or until filling is set and crust is golden. Cool completely in muffin cups on wire racks.
Makes about 4 dozen cookies

CANDY SHOP PIZZA

1½ cups all-purpose flour
½ teaspoon baking soda
½ teaspoon salt
10 tablespoons (1¼ sticks) butter, softened
½ cup granulated sugar
½ cup firmly packed brown sugar
1 egg
½ teaspoon vanilla extract
2 cups (12-ounce package) NESTLÉ® Toll House® Semi-Sweet Chocolate Morsels, divided

½ cup peanut butter
About 1 cup cut-up fruit, such as bananas and strawberries (optional)
About 1 cup chopped candy bars, such as NESTLÉ® CRUNCH® bars, BUTTERFINGER® bars, ALPINE WHITE® bars, GOOBERS® and RAISINETS®

Preheat oven to 375°F. In small bowl, combine flour, baking soda and salt; set aside.

In large mixer bowl, beat butter, granulated sugar and brown sugar until light and fluffy. Beat in egg and vanilla extract. Gradually beat in flour mixture. Stir in 1 cup morsels. Spread batter in lightly greased 12- to 14-inch pizza pan or 15½×10½-inch jelly-roll pan. Bake 20 to 24 minutes or until lightly browned.

Immediately sprinkle remaining 1 cup morsels over crust; drop peanut butter by spoonfuls onto morsels. Let stand 5 minutes or until soft and shiny. Gently spread chocolate and peanut butter over crust. Top with fruit and candy. Cut into wedges. Serve warm. *Makes about 12 servings*

PEANUT BUTTER JEWELS

1 package DUNCAN HINES® Peanut Butter Cookie Mix
1 egg
¼ cup sugar

¼ cup cocktail peanuts, finely chopped
Strawberry jam or apricot preserves

1. Preheat oven to 375°F.

2. Combine cookie mix, peanut butter flavor packet from Mix and egg in large bowl. Stir until thoroughly blended. Shape dough into 36 (1-inch) balls. Roll half the balls in sugar and half in chopped peanuts. Place 2 inches apart on ungreased baking sheets. Make indentation in center of each ball with finger or handle end of wooden spoon. Fill each with ¼ teaspoon strawberry jam. Bake at 375°F for 8 to 10 minutes or until light golden brown. Cool 1 minute on baking sheets. Remove to cooling racks. Cool completely. Store in airtight container. *Makes 3 dozen cookies*

Tip: For a delicious flavor variation, try seedless red raspberry or blackberry jam.

Candy Shop Pizza

Special Chocolate Chip Sandwiches

SPECIAL CHOCOLATE CHIP SANDWICHES

1 package DUNCAN HINES®
   Chocolate Chip Cookie Mix
1 egg
2 teaspoons water

8 ounces chocolate-flavored candy
   coating
¼ cup chopped sliced natural
   almonds

1. Preheat oven to 375°F. Combine cookie mix, contents of buttery flavor packet from Mix, egg and water in large bowl. Stir until thoroughly blended. Drop by rounded teaspoonfuls 2 inches apart onto ungreased baking sheets. Bake at 375°F for 8 to 10 minutes or until light golden brown. Cool 1 minute on baking sheets. Remove to cooling racks. Cool completely.

2. Place chocolate candy coating in small saucepan. Melt on low heat, stirring frequently until smooth.

3. To assemble, spread about ½ teaspoon melted coating on bottom of one cookie; top with second cookie. Press together to make sandwiches. Repeat with remaining cookies. Dip one-third of each sandwich cookie in remaining melted coating and sprinkle with almonds. Place on cooling racks until coating is set. Store between layers of waxed paper in airtight containers.

Makes 18 sandwich cookies

PINECONE COOKIES

6 tablespoons butter or margarine
⅓ cup HERSHEY'S Cocoa
1 cup sugar
2 eggs
1 teaspoon vanilla extract
2 cups all-purpose flour

½ teaspoon baking powder
½ teaspoon salt
¼ teaspoon baking soda
Light corn syrup
Sliced almonds

In small saucepan, melt butter over low heat; remove from heat. Add cocoa; blend well. In large mixer bowl, combine sugar, eggs and vanilla; blend in cocoa mixture. Stir together flour, baking powder, salt and baking soda in small bowl; add to cocoa-sugar mixture, beating until smooth. Refrigerate dough about 1 hour or until firm enough to roll.

Heat oven to 350°F. Roll out small portion of dough between two pieces of waxed paper to ⅛-inch thickness. Cut into pinecone shapes using 2- or 2½-inch oval cookie cutter. Place on lightly greased cookie sheets; lightly brush cookies with corn syrup. Arrange almonds in pinecone fashion; lightly drizzle or brush almonds with corn syrup. Repeat with remaining dough. Bake 7 to 8 minutes or until set. Cool slightly; remove from cookie sheets to wire racks. Cool completely.

Makes about 4 dozen cookies

ALMOND–RASPBERRY THUMBPRINT COOKIES

1 cup butter or margarine, softened
1 cup sugar
1 can SOLO® *or* 1 jar BAKER®
   Almond Filling
2 egg yolks
1 teaspoon almond extract

2½ cups all-purpose flour
½ teaspoon baking powder
½ teaspoon salt
1 can SOLO® *or* 1 jar BAKER®
   Raspberry or Strawberry Filling

Beat butter and sugar in medium bowl with electric mixer until light and fluffy. Add almond filling, egg yolks and almond extract; beat until blended. Stir in flour, baking powder and salt with wooden spoon to make soft dough. Cover; refrigerate at least 3 hours or overnight.

Preheat oven to 350°F. Shape dough into 1-inch balls. Place on ungreased baking sheets, about 1½ inches apart. Press thumb into center of each ball to make indentation. Spoon ½ teaspoon raspberry filling into each indentation. Bake 11 to 13 minutes or until edges of cookies are golden brown. Cool on baking sheets 1 minute. Remove from baking sheets; cool completely on wire racks.

Makes about 5 dozen cookies

Top to bottom: Anise Stars (page 167); Rum Raisin Balls (page 167); Noel Tarts (page 167); Chocolate-Frosted Almond Bars (page 167)

Festive
HOLIDAY COOKIES

Holiday Specialties   *160*

Cookie Exchanges   *174*

Creative Cutouts   *188*

Cookie Jar Classics   *204*

Brownie & Bar Greats   *216*

Holiday Specialties

DOUBLE CRUNCH BISCOTTI

⅓ cup vegetable oil
¾ cup sugar
3 eggs, beaten
½ teaspoon almond extract
½ teaspoon vanilla extract
2½ cups all-purpose flour

2 cups HONEY ALMOND DELIGHT®
   brand cereal, crushed to 1 cup
2 teaspoons baking powder
12 ounces chocolate, melted
   (optional)
¼ cup chopped almonds (optional)

Preheat oven to 350°F. Lightly grease cookie sheets. In large bowl, combine oil and sugar. Beat in eggs, almond extract and vanilla. Gradually stir in flour, cereal and baking powder. Divide dough in half. Place each half of dough on prepared cookie sheets; shape each into a 3½-inch by 11-inch log. Bake 25 to 28 minutes or until lightly browned. Remove from oven; immediately cut into ½-inch-thick slices. Place slices, cut side down, on clean ungreased cookie sheets. Bake 13 minutes, turning cookies over after 8 minutes. Cool on wire racks. If desired, spread chocolate on one end of each cookie; sprinkle with almonds.

Makes 44 cookies

Top to bottom: Frosty Cherry Cookies (page 163); Double Crunch Biscotti; Snow Puff Cookies (page 163)

ALMOND CREAM COOKIES

¾ cup (1½ sticks) margarine, softened
¾ cup granulated sugar
½ cup plus 2 tablespoons soft-style cream cheese
1 egg
1 teaspoon almond extract

1¼ cups all-purpose flour
¾ cup QUAKER® Corn Meal
½ teaspoon baking powder
½ cup coarsely chopped almonds
1 cup powdered sugar
1 tablespoon milk or water
Red or green candied cherries

Preheat oven to 350°F. Beat margarine, granulated sugar and ½ cup cream cheese at medium speed of electric mixer until light and fluffy. Add egg and almond extract; mix until well blended. Gradually add combined flour, corn meal and baking powder; mix well. Stir in almonds. Drop by rounded teaspoonfuls onto ungreased cookie sheets. Bake 12 to 14 minutes or until edges are golden brown. Cool on cookie sheets for 2 minutes; remove to wire racks. Cool completely.

Mix remaining 2 tablespoons cream cheese and powdered sugar until blended. Add milk; mix until smooth. Spread over cookies. Garnish with halved red or green candied cherries, if desired. Store tightly covered.   *Makes about 4 dozen cookies*

Almond Cream Cookies

FROSTY CHERRY COOKIES

½ cup (1 stick) butter or margarine
1 cup plus 3 tablespoons sugar,
  divided
1 egg, slightly beaten
½ teaspoon almond extract
1½ cups all-purpose flour
½ teaspoon salt

½ teaspoon baking soda
½ teaspoon baking powder
2 cups Rice CHEX® brand cereal,
  crushed to 1 cup
½ cup chopped green and red glacé
  cherries

Preheat oven to 350°F. In large bowl, combine butter and 1 cup sugar. Stir in egg and almond extract. Stir in flour, salt, baking soda and baking powder; mix well. Stir in cereal and cherries. Shape into ¾-inch balls. In small bowl, place remaining 3 tablespoons sugar. Roll balls in sugar. Place, 2 inches apart, on ungreased baking sheets. Bake 8 to 10 minutes or until bottoms are lightly browned.

Makes 6 dozen cookies

SNOW PUFF COOKIES

1 cup (2 sticks) butter or margarine,
  softened
1 cup sifted confectioners' sugar
2 teaspoons vanilla
2 cups all-purpose flour

1 cup Wheat CHEX® brand cereal,
  crushed to ⅓ cup
½ teaspoon salt
  Confectioners' sugar

Preheat oven to 325°F. In large bowl, combine butter and 1 cup sugar until well blended. Stir in vanilla. Stir in flour, cereal and salt, mixing well. Shape into 1-inch balls. Place, 2 inches apart, on ungreased baking sheets. Bake 14 to 16 minutes or until bottoms are lightly browned. Cool. Roll in confectioners' sugar.

Makes 3 dozen cookies

CHOCOLATE–DIPPED ALMOND HORNS

1½ cups powdered sugar
1 cup butter or margarine, softened
2 egg yolks
1½ teaspoons vanilla
2 cups all-purpose flour
½ cup ground almonds

1 teaspoon cream of tartar
1 teaspoon baking soda
1 cup semisweet chocolate chips,
    melted
Powdered sugar

Preheat oven to 325°F. In large mixer bowl, combine powdered sugar and butter. Beat at medium speed, scraping bowl often, until creamy, 1 to 2 minutes. Add egg yolks and vanilla; continue beating until well blended, 1 to 2 minutes. Reduce speed to low. Add flour, almonds, cream of tartar and baking soda. Continue beating, scraping bowl often, until well mixed, 1 to 2 minutes. Shape into 1-inch balls. Roll balls into 2-inch ropes; shape into crescents. Place, 2 inches apart, on cookie sheets. Flatten slightly with glass bottom covered in waxed paper. Bake for 8 to 10 minutes or until set. (Cookies do not brown.) Cool completely. Dip half of each cookie into chocolate; sprinkle remaining half with powdered sugar. Refrigerate until set.   *Makes about 3 dozen cookies*

CHERRY DOT COOKIES

2¼ cups all-purpose flour
2 teaspoons baking powder
½ teaspoon salt
¾ cup margarine, softened
1 cup sugar
2 eggs
2 tablespoons skim milk
1 teaspoon vanilla

1 cup chopped nuts
1 cup finely cut pitted dates
⅓ cup finely chopped maraschino
    cherries
2⅔ cups KELLOGG'S® CORN FLAKES®
    cereal, crushed to 1⅓ cups
15 maraschino cherries, cut into
    quarters

1. Preheat oven to 350°F. Stir together flour, baking powder and salt in small bowl. Set aside.

2. In large mixing bowl, beat margarine and sugar until light and fluffy. Add eggs. Beat well. Stir in milk and vanilla. Add flour mixture. Mix well. Stir in nuts, dates and ⅓ cup chopped cherries.

3. Shape level measuring tablespoons of dough into balls. Roll in Kellogg's® Corn Flakes® cereal. Place on cookie sheets coated with cooking spray. Top each cookie with cherry quarter.

4. Bake about 12 minutes or until lightly browned.   *Makes about 5 dozen cookies*

Chocolate-Dipped Almond Horns

Top to bottom: Anise Stars; Rum Raisin Balls; Noel Tarts; Chocolate-Frosted Almond Bars

HOLIDAY SHORTBREAD WITH VARIATIONS

1 cup (2 sticks) butter
½ cup sugar

2½ cups all-purpose flour
¼ teaspoon salt

Preheat oven to 375°F. Beat butter in large mixer bowl until fluffy. Add sugar; beat until light and fluffy. Gradually blend in flour and salt. Roll out on lightly floured surface to 11×7-inch rectangle, ½ inch thick. Cut into 1-inch squares. Bake on ungreased cookie sheets 12 to 15 minutes or until a pale golden color. Cool completely on wire racks. Store at room temperature in container with tight fitting lid.

Makes about 6 dozen

Variations

Anise Stars: Prepare Basic Shortbread, stirring in ¾ teaspoon anise extract and ¼ teaspoon nutmeg with flour and salt. Wrap dough in plastic wrap. Refrigerate 1 to 2 hours. Roll dough to ¼-inch thickness on lightly floured surface. Cut into star shape using floured cutter. Bake in preheated 375°F oven on ungreased cookie sheets 13 to 15 minutes or until very pale golden color. Cool completely on wire racks. Decorate with red and green frosting and small silver dragées. Makes 3 to 4 dozen.

Rum Raisin Balls: Prepare Basic Shortbread, stirring in 1 cup golden seedless raisins and 1 teaspoon rum extract with flour and salt. Form into 1-inch balls. Bake in preheated 375°F oven on ungreased cookie sheets 15 to 18 minutes or until pale golden color. Remove from cookie sheets; cool completely on wire racks. Dust lightly with confectioners' sugar before serving. Makes 5 dozen.

Noel Tarts: Prepare Basic Shortbread, stirring in 1 teaspoon vanilla extract with flour and salt. Press rounded tablespoonfuls of dough into 1¾-inch muffin cups. Bake in preheated 375°F oven 18 to 20 minutes or until pale golden in color. Cool in pan 10 minutes. Carefully remove from pan; cool completely on wire racks. Fill as desired with pie filling, pudding, mincemeat, etc. Makes 3 dozen.

Chocolate-Frosted Almond Bars: Prepare Basic Shortbread, reducing flour to 2 cups. Add ½ cup finely ground almonds and 1 teaspoon almond extract with flour and salt. Press into ungreased 13×9-inch baking pan. Bake in preheated 375°F oven 20 to 25 minutes or until pale golden color. Cool completely in pan on wire rack. Frost with 1 package (6 ounces) semisweet chocolate morsels, melted and combined with ½ cup dairy sour cream and 1 teaspoon vanilla extract. Cut into bars. Decorate with sliced almonds. Makes 4 dozen.

Favorite recipe from American Dairy Industry Association

DOUBLE SURPRISE COOKIES

⅔ cup butter or margarine
⅓ cup sugar
2 egg yolks
½ teaspoon vanilla
⅛ teaspoon almond extract
1½ cups all-purpose flour
¼ teaspoon salt

36 "M&M's"® Peanut, Peanut Butter or
    Almond Chocolate Candies
¼ cup confectioners' sugar
1½ teaspoons water
¾ cup "M&M's"® Semi-Sweet
    Chocolate Candies*

Preheat oven to 350°F. In mixer, beat butter 30 seconds. Gradually add sugar; beat until light and fluffy. Add egg yolks, vanilla and almond extract; beat thoroughly. Stir together flour and salt. Add to creamed mixture; mix well. Cover and chill at least 1 hour. For each cookie, shape, with floured hands, a rounded teaspoonful dough around each Peanut, Peanut Butter or Almond "M&M's"® to form a ball, about 1 inch in diameter. Place, 1 inch apart, on ungreased baking sheet. Bake 12 to 15 minutes until dough springs back when touched and cookie is lightly browned on bottom. Remove to wire racks; cool completely. To decorate, mix together confectioners' sugar and water until smooth. Spread on tops of cookies; immediately sprinkle generously with "M&M's"® Semi-Sweet Chocolate Candies, pressing in lightly.   *Makes 36 cookies*

*Found in baking section.

PEPPERMINT MACAROONS

2 egg whites
1 cup sugar
2 cups KELLOGG'S® SPECIAL K®
    cereal
½ cup (about 4 ounces) peppermint
    candy canes, crushed (about 5
    candy canes)

½ teaspoon vanilla
Vegetable cooking spray

1. In the bowl of an electric mixer, beat egg whites until foamy. Gradually add sugar, beating until stiff and glossy.

2. Add Kellogg's® Special K® cereal, candy canes and vanilla, mixing until blended. Drop by rounded teaspoonfuls onto baking sheets lightly coated with cooking spray.

3. Bake at 350°F about 12 minutes. Remove immediately from baking sheets. Let cool on wire racks. Store in airtight container.   *Makes about 3½ dozen cookies*

Kolacky

KOLACKY

½ cup butter or margarine, softened
3 ounces cream cheese, softened
1 teaspoon vanilla
1 cup all-purpose flour
⅛ teaspoon salt

6 teaspoons fruit preserves, assorted
   flavors
1 egg
1 teaspoon cold water
Powdered sugar (optional)

Combine butter and cream cheese in large bowl; beat until smooth and creamy. Blend in vanilla. Combine flour and salt; gradually add to butter mixture, mixing until mixture forms soft dough. Divide dough in half; wrap each half in plastic wrap. Refrigerate until firm.

Preheat oven to 375°F. Roll out half of dough on lightly floured pastry cloth or board to ⅛-inch thickness. Cut with top of glass or biscuit cutter into 3-inch rounds. Spoon ½ teaspoon preserves onto center of each dough circle. Beat egg with water; lightly brush onto edges of dough circles. Bring three edges of dough up over fruit spread; pinch edges together to seal. Place on ungreased cookie sheets; brush with egg mixture. Repeat with remaining dough, fruit spread and egg mixture. Bake 12 minutes or until golden brown. Let stand on cookie sheets 1 minute; transfer to wire racks. Cool completely. Sprinkle with powdered sugar, if desired. Store in tightly covered container.

Makes 2 dozen

Counter-clockwise from top: Peppermint Refrigerator Slices (page 172); Lemon Pecan Crescents (page 173); Spritz Christmas Trees; Peanut Butter Stars

SPRITZ CHRISTMAS TREES

⅓ cup (3½ ounces) almond paste
1 egg
1 package DUNCAN HINES® Golden
    Sugar Cookie Mix

8 drops green food coloring
1 container DUNCAN HINES® Creamy
    Homestyle Vanilla Frosting
Cinnamon candies, for garnish

1. Preheat oven to 375°F.

2. Combine almond paste and egg in large bowl. Beat at low speed with electric mixer until blended. Add contents of buttery flavor packet from Mix and green food coloring. Beat until smooth and evenly tinted. Add cookie mix. Beat at low speed until thoroughly blended.

3. Fit cookie press with Christmas tree plate; fill with dough. Force dough through press, 2 inches apart, onto ungreased cookie sheets. Bake at 375°F for 6 to 7 minutes or until set but not browned. Cool 1 minute on cookie sheets. Remove to cooling racks. Cool completely.

4. To decorate, fill resealable plastic bag half full with Vanilla frosting. Do not seal bag. Cut pinpoint hole in bottom corner of bag. Pipe small dot of frosting onto tip of one cookie tree and top with cinnamon candy. Repeat with remaining cookies. Pipe remaining frosting to form garland on cookie trees. Allow frosting to set before storing between layers of waxed paper in airtight container.

Makes about 5 dozen cookies

PEANUT BUTTER STARS

1 package DUNCAN HINES® Peanut
    Butter Cookie Mix
1 egg
2 packages (3½ ounces each)
    chocolate sprinkles

2 packages (7 ounces each) milk
    chocolate candy stars

1. Preheat oven to 375°F.

2. Combine cookie mix, contents of peanut butter packet from Mix and egg in large bowl. Stir until thoroughly blended. Shape dough into ¾-inch balls. Roll in chocolate sprinkles. Place, 2 inches apart, on ungreased cookie sheets. Bake at 375°F for 8 to 9 minutes or until set. Immediately place milk chocolate candy stars on top of hot cookies. Cool 1 minute on cookie sheets. Remove to cooling racks. Cool completely. Store in airtight containers.

Makes 7½ to 8 dozen cookies

PEPPERMINT REFRIGERATOR SLICES

3 packages DUNCAN HINES® Golden
   Sugar Cookie Mix, divided
3 eggs, divided
3 to 4 drops red food coloring

¾ teaspoon peppermint extract,
   divided
3 to 4 drops green food coloring

1. **For pink cookie dough,** combine contents of one buttery flavor packet from Mix, one egg, red food coloring and ¼ teaspoon peppermint extract in large bowl. Stir until evenly tinted. Add one cookie mix and stir until thoroughly blended. Set aside.

2. **For green cookie dough,** combine contents of one buttery flavor packet from Mix, one egg, ¼ teaspoon peppermint extract and green food coloring in large bowl. Stir until evenly tinted. Add one cookie mix and stir until thoroughly blended. Set aside.

3. **For plain cookie dough,** combine remaining cookie mix, contents of buttery flavor packet from Mix, egg and ¼ teaspoon peppermint extract in large bowl. Stir until thoroughly blended.

4. **To assemble,** divide each batch of cookie dough into four equal portions. Shape each portion into 12-inch-long roll on waxed paper. Lay one pink roll beside one green roll; press together slightly. Place one plain roll on top. Press rolls together to form one tri-colored roll; wrap in waxed paper or plastic wrap. Repeat with remaining rolls to form three more tri-colored rolls; wrap separately in waxed paper or plastic wrap. Refrigerate rolls for several hours or overnight.

5. Preheat oven to 375°F.

6. Cut chilled rolls into ¼-inch-thick slices. Place, 2 inches apart, on ungreased cookie sheets. Bake at 375°F for 7 to 8 minutes or until set but not browned. Cool 1 minute on cookie sheets. Remove to cooling racks. Cool completely. Store in airtight containers.   *Makes about 15 dozen small cookies*

CHERRY THUMBPRINT COOKIES

¾ cup sugar
½ cup HELLMANN'S® or BEST FOODS®
   Real Mayonnaise
½ cup MAZOLA® Margarine
2 eggs, separated
1 teaspoon vanilla

2 cups all-purpose flour
¼ teaspoon ground nutmeg
1½ cups finely chopped walnuts or
   almonds
   Red and green candied cherries

In large bowl, beat sugar, mayonnaise, margarine, egg yolks and vanilla. Beat in flour and nutmeg until well blended. Cover; refrigerate until firm, at least 3 hours.

Preheat oven to 350°F. Shape dough into ¾-inch balls. In small bowl, beat egg whites with fork until foamy. Dip each ball into egg whites; roll in nuts. Place, 1½ inches apart, on greased cookie sheets. Press thumb into centers of balls. Place one whole cherry in each center. Bake 15 to 17 minutes or until bottoms are browned. Let cookies cool slightly before removing them from cookie sheets to wire racks.

Makes about 5 dozen cookies

LEMON PECAN CRESCENTS

1 package DUNCAN HINES® Golden
   Sugar Cookie Mix
2 egg whites
¾ cup toasted pecans, chopped

¼ cup all-purpose flour
1 tablespoon grated lemon peel
Confectioners' sugar

1. Preheat oven to 375°F.

2. Combine cookie mix, contents of buttery flavor packet from Mix, egg whites, pecans, flour and lemon peel in large bowl. Stir until thoroughly blended. Form level ½ measuring tablespoonfuls dough into crescent shapes. Place, 2 inches apart, on ungreased baking sheets. Bake at 375°F for 7 to 8 minutes or until set but not browned. Cool 2 minutes on baking sheets. Remove to cooling racks. Roll warm cookies in confectioners' sugar. Cool completely. Roll cookies again in confectioners' sugar. Store between layers of waxed paper in airtight container.

Makes about 5 dozen cookies

DATE–NUT MACAROONS

1 (8-ounce) package pitted dates,
   chopped
1½ cups flaked coconut
1 cup PLANTERS® Pecan Halves,
   chopped

¾ cup sweetened condensed milk
   (not evaporated milk)
½ teaspoon vanilla extract

Preheat oven to 350°F.

In medium bowl, combine dates, coconut and nuts; blend in sweetened condensed milk and vanilla. Drop by rounded tablespoonfuls onto greased and floured cookie sheets. Bake for 10 to 12 minutes or until light golden brown. Carefully remove from cookie sheets; cool completely on wire racks. Store in airtight container.

Makes about 2 dozen cookies

Cookie Exchanges

CHERRY RUM COOKIES

4 cups KELLOGG'S® SPECIAL K®
cereal, crushed to 1½ cups,
divided
2¼ cups all-purpose flour
1 teaspoon baking powder
¼ teaspoon salt (optional)

½ cup margarine, softened
⅔ cup sugar
1 egg
1 teaspoon rum flavoring
10 to 12 maraschino cherries, cut into
quarters

1. Stir together 1 cup of the crushed Kellogg's® Special K® cereal, flour, baking powder and salt in medium bowl. Set aside.

2. In large mixing bowl, beat margarine and sugar until light and fluffy. Add egg and rum flavoring. Beat well. Add dry ingredients. Mix well.

3. Shape dough into balls using rounded measuring teaspoon. Roll in remaining ½ cup crushed cereal. Place on ungreased baking sheets. Top each cookie with cherry quarter.

4. Bake at 375°F about 12 minutes or until lightly browned. Remove immediately from baking sheets. Cool on wire racks. Store in airtight container.

Makes 3½ dozen

Top to bottom: Corn Flake Macaroons (page 177); Cherry Rum Cookies

CHOCOLATE–DIPPED BRANDY SNAPS

½ cup butter
½ cup sugar
⅓ cup dark corn syrup
½ teaspoon cinnamon
¼ teaspoon ginger
 1 cup all-purpose flour

2 teaspoons brandy
1 cup (6-ounce package) NESTLÉ®
   Toll House® Semi-Sweet
   Chocolate Morsels
1 tablespoon vegetable shortening
⅓ cup finely chopped nuts

Preheat oven to 300°F. In heavy saucepan, combine butter, sugar, dark corn syrup, cinnamon and ginger; cook over medium heat, stirring constantly, until melted and smooth. Remove from heat; stir in flour and brandy. Drop mixture by rounded teaspoonfuls, about 3 inches apart, onto ungreased cookie sheets. (Do not bake more than 6 cookies at one time.)

Bake at 300°F for 10 to 12 minutes. Let stand a few seconds. Remove from cookie sheets and immediately roll around wooden spoon handle; cool completely. Combine over hot, not boiling, water, morsels and vegetable shortening; stir until morsels are melted and mixture is smooth. Dip each Brandy Snap halfway into melted chocolate. Sprinkle with nuts; set on waxed paper-lined cookie sheets. Chill until set. Store in airtight container in refrigerator.   *Makes about 3 dozen (2½-inch) snaps*

Chocolate-Dipped Brandy Snaps

CORN FLAKE MACAROONS

4 egg whites
1 teaspoon vanilla
¼ teaspoon cream of tartar
1⅓ cups sugar

1 cup chopped pecans
1 cup shredded coconut
3 cups KELLOGG'S® CORN FLAKES®
cereal

1. Preheat oven to 325°F. In large mixing bowl, beat egg whites until foamy. Stir in vanilla and cream of tartar. Gradually add sugar, beating until stiff and glossy. Fold in pecans, coconut and Kellogg's® Corn Flakes® cereal. Drop mixture by rounded measuring tablespoons onto cookie sheets sprayed with vegetable cooking spray.

2. Bake about 15 minutes or until lightly browned. Remove immediately from cookie sheets. Cool on wire racks.   *Makes about 3 dozen cookies*

Variation: Fold in ½ cup crushed peppermint candy with pecans and coconut.

RASPBERRY ALMOND SANDWICH COOKIES

1 package DUNCAN HINES® Golden
   Sugar Cookie Mix
1 egg
1 tablespoon water

½ teaspoon almond extract
¾ cup sliced natural almonds, broken
   Seedless red raspberry jam

1. Preheat oven to 375°F.

2. Combine cookie mix, buttery flavor packet from Mix, egg, water and almond extract in large bowl. Stir until thoroughly blended. Drop half the dough by level measuring teaspoons, 2 inches apart, onto ungreased cookie sheets. (It is a small amount of dough but will spread during baking to 1½ to 1¾ inches.)

3. Place almonds on waxed paper. Drop other half of dough by level measuring teaspoons onto nuts. Place, almond-side up, 2 inches apart on cookie sheets.

4. Bake both plain and almond cookies at 375°F for 6 minutes or until set but not browned. Cool 1 minute on cookie sheets. Remove to cooling racks. Cool completely.

5. Spread bottoms of plain cookies with jam; top with almond cookies. Press together to make sandwiches. Store in airtight container.   *Makes 4½ to 5 dozen cookies*

NO–BAKE PEANUTTY COOKIES

2 cups Roasted Honey Nut SKIPPY®
    Creamy or SUPER CHUNK®
    Peanut Butter
2 cups graham cracker crumbs
1 cup confectioners' sugar

½ cup KARO® Light or Dark Corn
    Syrup
¼ cup semisweet chocolate chips,
    melted
Colored sprinkles (optional)

In large bowl, combine peanut butter, graham cracker crumbs, confectioners' sugar and corn syrup. Mix until smooth. Shape into 1-inch balls. Place on waxed paper-lined cookie sheets. Drizzle melted chocolate over balls or roll in colored sprinkles. Store covered in refrigerator.

Makes about 5 dozen cookies

MELTING MOMENTS

1 cup flour
½ cup ARGO® or KINGSFORD'S® Corn
    Starch

½ cup confectioners' sugar
¾ cup MAZOLA® Margarine, softened
1 teaspoon vanilla

In medium bowl, combine flour, corn starch and confectioners' sugar. In large bowl with mixer at medium speed, beat margarine until smooth. Add flour mixture and vanilla; beat until well blended. If necessary, refrigerate dough 1 hour or until easy to handle.

Preheat oven to 350°F. Shape dough into 1-inch balls. Place, 1½ inches apart, on ungreased cookie sheets; flatten with lightly floured fork. Bake 10 to 12 minutes or until edges are lightly browned. Remove from cookie sheets; cool completely on wire racks. Store in tightly covered container.

Makes about 3 dozen cookies

Almond Melting Moments: Add 1 cup finely chopped almonds to flour mixture.

Food Processor Method: In bowl of food processor with metal blade, combine flour, corn starch and confectioners' sugar. Cut cold margarine into 1-inch pieces. Add to flour mixture. Process, adding vanilla through feed tube, 15 seconds or until mixture forms a ball. Continue as above.

CHOCOLATE CHIP & MINT MERINGUE COOKIES

3 egg whites
½ teaspoon cream of tartar
    Pinch of salt
¾ cup sugar

4 drops green food coloring
4 drops mint extract
1 (6-ounce) package miniature
    semisweet chocolate chips

Preheat oven to 375°F. Grease and lightly flour two cookie sheets. In large bowl, beat egg whites with cream of tartar and salt until foamy. Gradually beat in sugar, 2 tablespoons at a time, until soft peaks form. Stir in food coloring and mint extract. Fold in chocolate chips. Drop meringue by teaspoonfuls, 1 inch apart, onto prepared cookie sheets. Place in preheated oven. Turn off heat; let meringues set in oven 8 to 12 hours.   *Makes about 4 dozen cookies*

Chocolate Chip & Mint Meringue Cookies

Choco-Cherry Cookies Supreme

CHOCO–CHERRY COOKIES SUPREME

⅔ cup all-purpose flour
½ cup unsweetened cocoa
1½ teaspoons baking powder
½ teaspoon salt
⅓ cup butter or margarine, softened
½ cup granulated sugar
½ cup packed light brown sugar
⅓ cup milk

1 large egg
1 teaspoon vanilla
2 cups uncooked quick-cooking or old-fashioned oats
3 ounces white baking bar *or* white chocolate candy bar, cut into ¼-inch pieces
½ cup candied cherries

Preheat oven to 375°F. Combine flour, cocoa, baking powder and salt in small bowl; set aside. Beat butter and both sugars in large bowl with electric mixer at medium speed until light and fluffy. Beat in milk, egg and vanilla, scraping down side of bowl once. Gradually add flour mixture. Stir in oats until well blended. Stir in baking bar pieces and cherries. Drop heaping teaspoonfuls of dough, 2 inches apart, onto greased cookie sheets. Bake 10 minutes or until set. Let stand on cookie sheets 1 minute. Remove cookies to wire racks; cool completely.

Makes about 3 dozen cookies

PECAN DROPS

¾ cup sugar
½ cup FLEISCHMANN'S® Margarine, softened
¼ cup EGG BEATERS® 99% Real Egg Product
1 teaspoon vanilla extract

2 cups all-purpose flour
⅔ cup PLANTERS® Pecans, finely chopped
3 tablespoons jam, jelly or preserves, any flavor

In small bowl, with electric mixer at medium speed, beat sugar and margarine. Add egg product and vanilla; beat for 1 minute. Stir in flour until blended. Chill dough for 1 hour.

Preheat oven to 350°F. Form dough into 36 (1¼-inch) balls; roll in pecans, pressing into dough. Place, 2 inches apart, on greased cookie sheets. Indent center of each ball with thumb or back of wooden spoon. Bake for 10 minutes; remove from oven. Spoon ¼ teaspoon jam into each cookie indentation. Bake for 2 to 5 more minutes or until lightly browned. Remove from sheets; cool on wire racks.

Makes about 3 dozen cookies

Chocolate Peanut Butter Cups

CHOCOLATE PEANUT BUTTER CUPS

1 cup semisweet chocolate chips
1½ cups firmly packed light brown
    sugar
⅔ cup CRISCO® All-Vegetable
    Shortening
1 tablespoon water
1 teaspoon vanilla
2 eggs

DRIZZLE
1 cup peanut butter chips

1½ cups all-purpose flour
⅓ cup unsweetened baking cocoa
½ teaspoon salt
¼ teaspoon baking soda
¾ cup finely chopped peanuts
36 miniature peanut butter cups,
    unwrapped

1. Heat oven to 375°F.

2. **For cookies,** place chocolate chips in microwave-safe measuring cup or bowl. Microwave at MEDIUM (50% power) 2 minutes; stir. Repeat until smooth. (Or, melt on rangetop in small saucepan on very low heat.) Cool slightly.

3. Combine brown sugar, shortening, water and vanilla in large bowl. Beat at medium speed of electric mixer until well blended. Beat eggs into shortening mixture. Reduce speed to low. Add chocolate slowly. Mix until well blended.

4. Combine flour, cocoa, salt and baking soda in medium bowl. Mix into shortening mixture at low speed just until blended.

5. Shape dough into 1¼-inch balls. Roll in nuts. Place 2 inches apart on ungreased baking sheets.

6. Bake at 375°F for 7 to 9 minutes or until set. Immediately press peanut butter cup into center of each cookie. Press sides of cookie up against cup. Cool 2 minutes on baking sheets. Remove to wire racks to cool completely.

7. **For drizzle,** place peanut butter chips in heavy resealable plastic food storage bag. Seal. Microwave at MEDIUM (50% power) 1 minute. Knead bag. Repeat until smooth. (Or, melt by placing bag in hot water.) Cut pinpoint hole in bottom corner of bag. Squeeze out and drizzle over cookies.

Makes about 3 dozen cookies

TOFFEE TASSIES

½ **cup margarine or butter**
1 **(3-ounce) package cream cheese,**
    softened
1 **cup all-purpose flour**
¼ **cup ground pecans**
¾ **cup packed brown sugar**

1 **egg**
1 **tablespoon margarine or butter,**
    melted
½ **cup chopped pecans**
½ **cup HEATH® Bits**

For pastry, in medium mixing bowl beat ½ cup margarine or butter and cream cheese until thoroughly combined. Stir in flour and ground pecans. Press a rounded teaspoon of pastry evenly into the bottom and up sides of 24 ungreased 1¾-inch miniature muffin cups. Set aside.

For filling, beat together brown sugar, egg and 1 tablespoon melted margarine or butter in small mixing bowl. Stir in chopped pecans. Spoon 1 teaspoon filling into each pastry-lined cup. Sprinkle about 1 teaspoon Heath® Bits over filling. Bake in 325°F oven about 30 minutes or until pastry is golden and filling is puffed. Cool slightly in pans on wire racks. Remove and cool completely on wire racks.

Makes 24 tassies

CHERRY COCONUT COOKIES

⅔ cup granulated sugar
½ cup BUTTER FLAVOR* CRISCO®
    All-Vegetable Shortening
1 egg
2 tablespoons light corn syrup or
    regular pancake syrup
¾ teaspoon almond extract
½ teaspoon vanilla
1 teaspoon grated lemon peel

1¾ cups all-purpose flour
½ teaspoon baking powder
¼ teaspoon baking soda
¼ teaspoon salt
¾ cup flaked coconut
½ cup coarsely chopped pecans
⅓ cup quartered maraschino
    cherries, well drained on paper
    towel

1. Heat oven to 350°F. Combine sugar and shortening in large bowl. Beat at medium speed of electric mixer until well blended. Add egg, corn syrup, almond extract, vanilla and lemon peel. Beat until light and fluffy.

2. Combine flour, baking powder, baking soda and salt in medium bowl. Gradually add to shortening mixture at low speed. Mix until well blended. Stir in coconut, nuts and cherries.

3. Shape dough into 1-inch balls. Place 2 inches apart on ungreased baking sheets. Bake at 350°F for 11 to 12 minutes. Cool 2 minutes on baking sheets. Remove to wire racks to cool completely.

Makes 3½ dozen cookies

*BUTTER FLAVOR CRISCO® is artificially flavored.

CREAM CHEESE COOKIES

½ cup BUTTER FLAVOR* CRISCO®
    All-Vegetable Shortening
1 package (3 ounces) cream cheese,
    softened
1 tablespoon milk

1 cup sugar
½ teaspoon vanilla
1 cup all-purpose flour
½ cup chopped pecans

1. Heat oven to 375°F. Combine shortening, cream cheese and milk in medium bowl. Beat at medium speed of electric mixer until well blended. Beat in sugar and vanilla. Mix in flour. Add nuts.

2. Drop dough by level measuring tablespoonfuls 2 inches apart onto ungreased baking sheets. Bake at 375°F for 10 minutes. Cool 2 minutes on baking sheets. Remove to wire racks to cool completely.

Makes about 3 dozen cookies

*BUTTER FLAVOR CRISCO® is artificially flavored.

Top to bottom: Cherry Coconut Cookies; Cream Cheese Cookies; Chocolate Thumbprints (page 186)

CHOCOLATE THUMBPRINTS

COOKIES

1½ cups firmly packed light brown
   sugar
⅔ cup CRISCO® All-Vegetable
   Shortening
1 tablespoon water
1 teaspoon vanilla

2 eggs
1½ cups all-purpose flour
⅓ cup unsweetened baking cocoa
½ teaspoon salt
¼ teaspoon baking soda
½ cup miniature chocolate chips

PEANUT BUTTER CREAM FILLING

⅓ cup creamy peanut butter
2 tablespoons BUTTER FLAVOR*
   CRISCO® All-Vegetable
   Shortening

1 cup confectioners' sugar
2 tablespoons milk
½ teaspoon vanilla

1. Heat oven to 375°F.

2. **For cookies,** combine brown sugar, ⅔ cup shortening, water and 1 teaspoon vanilla in large bowl. Beat at medium speed of electric mixer until well blended. Beat in eggs until well blended.

3. Combine flour, cocoa, salt and baking soda in medium bowl. Mix into shortening mixture at low speed just until blended. Stir in chocolate chips.

4. Shape dough into 1-inch balls. Place 2 inches apart on ungreased baking sheets. Press thumb gently into center of each cookie.

5. Bake at 375°F for 7 to 9 minutes or until set. Press centers again with small measuring spoon. Cool 2 minutes on baking sheets. Remove to wire racks to cool completely.

6. **For peanut butter cream filling,** combine peanut butter and 2 tablespoons shortening in medium bowl. Stir with spoon until blended. Add confectioners' sugar. Stir well. Add milk and ½ teaspoon vanilla. Stir until smooth. Spoon into centers of cookies.   *Makes about 3 dozen cookies*

*BUTTER FLAVOR CRISCO® is artificially flavored.

WALNUT JAM CRESCENTS

⅔ cup butter or margarine
1⅓ cups all-purpose flour
½ cup dairy sour cream
⅔ cup raspberry jam or orange
   marmalade, divided

⅔ cup DIAMOND® Walnuts, finely
   chopped, divided

Preheat oven to 350°F. In medium bowl, cut butter into flour until mixture resembles fine crumbs. Add sour cream; mix until stiff dough is formed. Divide dough in half. Shape each half into a ball; flatten slightly. Wrap balls in waxed paper; chill well. Working with one half of dough at a time, roll dough into 11-inch round on lightly floured pastry cloth or board. Spread with ⅓ cup jam; sprinkle with ⅓ cup walnuts. Cut into quarters; cut each quarter into three wedges. Roll up, one at a time, starting from outer edge; place on lightly greased cookie sheets. Repeat with remaining half of dough. Bake 25 to 30 minutes or until lightly browned. Remove to wire racks to cool.   *Makes about 2 dozen crescents*

AUSTRIAN TEA COOKIES

1½ cups sugar, divided
½ cup butter, softened
½ cup shortening
1 egg, beaten
½ teaspoon vanilla extract
2 cups all-purpose flour
2 cups HONEY ALMOND DELIGHT®
    Brand Cereal, crushed to 1 cup

½ teaspoon baking powder
¼ teaspoon ground cinnamon
14 ounces almond paste
2 egg whites
5 tablespoons raspberry or apricot
    jam, warmed

In large bowl, beat 1 cup sugar, butter and shortening. Add egg and vanilla; mix well. Stir in flour, cereal, baking powder and cinnamon until well blended. Refrigerate 1 to 2 hours or until firm.

Preheat oven to 350°F. Roll dough out on lightly floured surface to ¼-inch thickness; cut into 2-inch circles with floured cookie cutter. Place on ungreased cookie sheets; set aside.

In small bowl, beat almond paste, egg whites and remaining ½ cup sugar until smooth. With pastry tube fitted with medium-sized star tip, pipe almond paste mixture, ½ inch thick, along outside edge of top of each cookie. Spoon ¼ teaspoon jam into center of each cookie.

Bake 8 to 10 minutes or until lightly browned. Let stand 1 minute before removing from cookie sheets. Cool on wire racks.   *Makes about 3½ dozen cookies*

Creative Cutouts

FROSTED BUTTER COOKIES

COOKIES
1½ cups butter, softened
¾ cup granulated sugar
3 egg yolks
3 cups all-purpose flour

1 teaspoon baking powder
2 tablespoons orange juice
1 teaspoon vanilla

FROSTING
4 cups confectioners' sugar
½ cup butter, softened
3 to 4 tablespoons milk
2 teaspoons vanilla

Food coloring (optional)
Colored sugars, flaked coconut and
cinnamon candies for decoration

For Cookies, in large bowl, beat 1½ cups butter and granulated sugar. Add egg yolks; beat until light and fluffy. Add flour, baking powder, orange juice and 1 teaspoon vanilla; beat until well mixed. Cover; refrigerate until firm, 2 to 3 hours.

Preheat oven to 350°F. Roll out dough, one half at a time, to ¼-inch thickness on well-floured surface. Cut out with holiday cookie cutters. Place, 1 inch apart, on ungreased cookie sheets. Bake 6 to 10 minutes or until edges are golden brown. Remove to wire racks to cool completely.

For Frosting, in medium bowl, combine all frosting ingredients except food coloring and decorations; beat until light and fluffy. If desired, divide frosting into small bowls; tint with food coloring. Frost cookies and decorate with colored sugars, coconut and candies. *Makes about 3 dozen cookies*

Frosted Butter Cookies

Cinnamon Stars

CINNAMON STARS

2 tablespoons sugar
¾ teaspoon ground cinnamon
¾ cup butter or margarine, softened
2 egg yolks

1 teaspoon vanilla extract
1 package DUNCAN HINES® Moist
    Deluxe French Vanilla Cake Mix

1. Preheat oven to 375°F.

2. Combine sugar and cinnamon in small bowl. Set aside.

3. Combine butter, egg yolks and vanilla extract in large bowl. Blend in cake mix gradually. Roll to ⅛-inch thickness on lightly floured surface. Cut with 2½-inch star cookie cutter. Place, 2 inches apart, on ungreased cookie sheets. Sprinkle cookies with cinnamon-sugar mixture. Bake at 375°F for 6 to 8 minutes or until edges are light golden brown. Cool 1 minute on cookie sheets. Remove to cooling racks. Cool completely. Store in airtight container.

Makes 3 to 3½ dozen cookies

COCOA ALMOND CUTOUT COOKIES

¾ cup margarine or butter, softened
1 (14-ounce) can EAGLE® Brand
    Sweetened Condensed Milk (NOT
    evaporated milk)
2 eggs
1 teaspoon vanilla extract
½ teaspoon almond extract

2¾ cups unsifted flour
⅔ cup HERSHEY®S Cocoa
2 teaspoons baking powder
½ teaspoon baking soda
½ cup finely chopped almonds
    Chocolate Glaze (recipe follows)

In large mixer bowl, beat margarine, sweetened condensed milk, eggs and both extracts until well blended. Combine dry ingredients; add to margarine mixture. Beat until well blended. Stir in almonds. Divide dough into four equal portions. Wrap each in plastic wrap; flatten. Chill until firm enough to roll, about 2 hours.

Preheat oven to 350°F. Working with one portion at a time (keep remaining dough in refrigerator), on floured surface, roll to about ⅛-inch thickness. Cut into desired shapes. Place on lightly greased baking sheets. Bake 6 to 8 minutes or until set. Remove from baking sheets. Cool completely. Prepare Chocolate Glaze. Drizzle with glaze. Store tightly covered at room temperature.

Makes about 6 dozen (3-inch) cookies

Chocolate Glaze: Melt 1 cup (6 ounces) HERSHEY®S Semi-Sweet Chocolate Chips with 2 tablespoons shortening. Makes about ⅔ cup.

HOLIDAY GINGERBREAD PEOPLE

1 (14½-ounce) package gingerbread
    mix
⅓ cup orange juice
1 tablespoon grated orange peel
½ teaspoon ground cinnamon

1 cup confectioners' sugar
4 teaspoons milk
½ cup "M&M's"® Plain Chocolate
    Candies

Preheat oven to 375°F. In large mixing bowl, blend gingerbread mix, orange juice, orange peel and cinnamon until smooth. Turn dough onto floured surface; knead until smooth. Form into a ball; divide in half. Roll out half of dough to ⅛-inch thickness. With 6-inch cookie cutter, cut three or four cookie people, carefully placing on lightly greased baking sheets. Re-roll dough scraps; cut to make eight cookies in all. Repeat with remaining half of dough. Bake 6 to 8 minutes or until firm. Cool slightly; remove to wire racks to cool completely. Combine confectioners' sugar and milk; mix until well blended. Spoon into icing bag fitted with writing tip. Outline cookies with icing. Decorate with candies.

Makes 16 cookies

PEANUT BUTTER SUGAR COOKIES

1 6-ounce package (3 bars) NESTLÉ®
    Premier White® Baking Bars,
    divided
2½ cups all-purpose flour
¾ teaspoon salt
¾ cup (1½ sticks) butter or
    margarine, softened

¾ cup peanut butter
1 cup sugar
1 egg
1 teaspoon vanilla extract
    Assorted NESTLÉ® Toll House®
    Morsels

In small saucepan over low heat, melt 1 baking bar; set aside. In small bowl, combine flour and salt; set aside.

In large mixer bowl, beat butter, peanut butter and sugar until creamy. Blend in egg and vanilla extract. Beat in melted baking bar. Gradually beat in flour mixture. Divide dough in half. Shape each half into a ball. Wrap with plastic wrap. Refrigerate 3 to 4 hours until firm enough to roll.

Preheat oven to 350°F. Between two sheets of waxed paper, roll each ball to ⅛-inch thickness. Peel off top sheets of waxed paper; cut with 2½- to 3-inch cookie cutters. Slide waxed paper onto ungreased cookie sheets; refrigerate 10 minutes. Transfer cutouts to ungreased cookie sheets. Decorate with assorted morsels.

Bake 10 to 12 minutes until set. Let stand 2 minutes. Remove from cookie sheets; cool completely.

In small saucepan over low heat, melt remaining 2 baking bars. Drizzle over cookies.

Makes about 5 dozen cookies

BUTTER COOKIES

¾ cup butter, softened
¼ cup granulated sugar
¼ cup packed brown sugar
1 egg yolk

1¾ cups all-purpose flour
¾ teaspoon baking powder
⅛ teaspoon salt

1. Combine butter, both sugars and egg yolk in medium bowl. Add flour, baking powder and salt; mix well. Cover; chill until firm, about 4 hours or overnight.

2. Preheat oven to 350°F. Roll dough on floured surface to ¼-inch thickness. Cut into desired shapes with cookie cutters. Place on ungreased cookie sheets.

3. Bake 8 to 10 minutes or until edges begin to brown. Remove to wire racks; cool completely.

Makes about 2 dozen cookies

Peanut Butter Sugar Cookies

Kittens and Mittens

KITTENS AND MITTENS

Chocolate Cookie dough (page 195)   **Assorted food colors**
Cookie Glaze (page 195)   **Assorted candies**

1. Preheat oven to 325°F. Grease cookie sheets.

2. Prepare Chocolate Cookie dough. Roll dough on floured surface to ⅛-inch thickness. Using diagrams 1 and 2 (page 195) as guides, cut out kitten and mitten cookies. Place cookies on prepared cookie sheets. With plastic straw, make holes in tops of cookies, about ½ inch from top edges.

3. Bake 8 to 10 minutes or until edges begin to brown. Remove to wire racks; cool completely. If necessary, push straw through warm cookies to remake holes.

4. Prepare Cookie Glaze; set aside.

5. Place cookies on racks on waxed paper-lined baking sheets. Spoon glaze into several small bowls. Color as desired with food color. Spoon glaze over cookies. Place some of remaining colored glaze in small plastic food storage bag. Cut pinpoint hole in corner of bag. Use to pipe decorations as shown in photo. Decorate with candies as shown. Let stand until glaze has set.

6. Thread yarn or ribbon through holes to make garland.   *Makes about 2 dozen cookies*

CHOCOLATE COOKIES

1 cup butter or margarine, softened
1 cup sugar
1 egg
1 teaspoon vanilla
2 ounces semisweet chocolate,
    melted

2¼ cups all-purpose flour
1 teaspoon baking powder
¼ teaspoon salt

1. Beat butter and sugar in large bowl at high speed of electric mixer until light and fluffy. Beat in egg and vanilla. Add melted chocolate; mix well. Add flour, baking powder and salt; mix well. Cover; refrigerate until firm, about 2 hours.

2. Preheat oven to 325°F. Grease cookie sheets. Roll dough on floured surface to ⅛-inch thickness. Cut into desired shapes with cookie cutters. Place on prepared cookie sheets.

3. Bake 8 to 10 minutes or until set. Remove to wire racks; cool completely.

Makes about 3 dozen cookies

COOKIE GLAZE

4 cups confectioners' sugar
4 to 6 tablespoons milk

Assorted food color

1. Combine confectioners' sugar and enough milk to make a medium-thick pourable glaze. Color as desired with food color.

2. Place cookies on wire rack on waxed paper-lined baking sheet. Spoon glaze over cookies; allow to dry completely.

Makes about 4 cups glaze

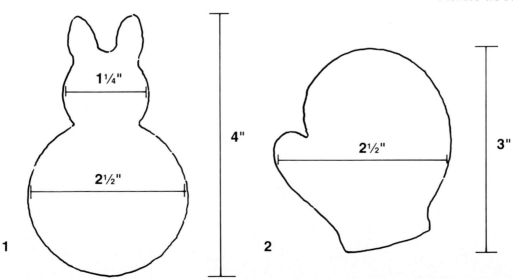

HANUKKAH COOKIES

COOKIES
¾ cup butter or margarine, softened
2 egg yolks
2 tablespoons grated orange peel

1 package DUNCAN HINES® Moist
Deluxe White Cake Mix

FROSTING
1 container (16 ounces) DUNCAN
HINES® Creamy Homestyle
Vanilla Frosting

3 to 4 drops blue food coloring
3 to 4 drops yellow food coloring

1. **For Cookies,** combine butter, egg yolks and orange peel in large bowl. Beat at low speed with electric mixer until blended. Add cake mix gradually, beating until thoroughly blended. Form dough into a ball. Cover with plastic wrap and refrigerate for 1 to 2 hours or until chilled but not firm.

2. Preheat oven to 375°F.

3. Roll dough to ⅛-inch thickness on lightly floured surface. Cut with Hanukkah cookie cutters. Place, 2 inches apart, on ungreased cookie sheets. Bake at 375°F for 6 to 7 minutes or until edges are light golden brown. Cool 1 minute on cookie sheets. Remove to cooling racks. Cool completely.

4. **For Frosting,** tint ½ cup Vanilla frosting with blue food coloring. Warm frosting in microwave oven at HIGH (100% power) for 5 to 10 seconds, if desired. Place writing tip on pastry bag. Fill with tinted frosting. Pipe outline pattern on cookies (see photo). Tint ½ cup frosting with yellow food coloring and leave ½ cup frosting untinted; decorate as desired. Allow frosting to set before storing cookies between layers of waxed paper in airtight container.   *Makes 3½ to 4 dozen cookies*

Hanukkah Cookies

Chocolate Gingerbread Cookies

CHOCOLATE GINGERBREAD COOKIES

COOKIES
2¼ cups all-purpose flour
¾ cup NESTLÉ® Cocoa
1 teaspoon baking soda
1 teaspoon ginger
½ teaspoon baking powder
½ teaspoon cinnamon
½ teaspoon cloves

¼ teaspoon salt
½ cup (1 stick) butter or margarine, softened
1 cup granulated sugar
1 egg
½ cup molasses

GLAZE
1 cup confectioners' sugar
2 to 3 tablespoons milk

1 bar (2 ounces) NESTLÉ® Semi-Sweet Chocolate Baking Bar, broken up

Cookies: In small bowl, combine flour, cocoa, baking soda, ginger, baking powder, cinnamon, cloves and salt; set aside.

In large mixer bowl, beat butter and granulated sugar until creamy. Blend in egg and molasses. Gradually beat in flour mixture. Divide dough into four equal pieces; wrap in plastic wrap. Refrigerate at least 2 hours until firm.

Preheat oven to 350°F. Lightly grease two large cookie sheets. On floured board, roll dough, one piece at a time, to ⅛-inch thickness. Cut with 4½-inch cookie cutters. With metal spatula, transfer cutouts to prepared cookie sheets. Repeat with remaining dough.

Bake 8 to 10 minutes until set. Let stand 2 minutes. Remove from cookie sheets; cool completely.

Glaze: In small bowl, combine confectioners' sugar and 2 tablespoons milk; stir until smooth. (Add additional 1 tablespoon milk if necessary for desired consistency.) Set aside.

In small saucepan over low heat, melt baking bar. Pipe cookies with Glaze or decorate with melted baking bar.   *Makes about 2 dozen cookies*

CHRISTMAS STAINED GLASS COOKIES

Hard candies (in assorted colors)	**3 cups all-purpose flour**
¾ cup butter, softened	**1 teaspoon baking powder**
¾ cup white granulated sugar	**Frosting (optional)**
2 eggs	**Candy (optional)**
1 teaspoon vanilla	

Separate colors of hard candy. Place each color of candy in small freezer-weight plastic food storage bag; crush with a wooden mallet.* In large mixing bowl, beat together butter and sugar. Beat in eggs and vanilla. Combine flour and baking powder in medium bowl. Gradually stir into butter mixture until dough is very stiff. Wrap in plastic wrap; chill about 3 hours.

Preheat oven to 375°F. Roll out dough to ⅛-inch thickness on lightly floured surface. Additional flour can be added, if necessary. Cut out cookies using large Christmas cookie cutters. Transfer cookies to foil-lined baking sheet. Using small Christmas cookie cutter of the same shape as the large one, cut out and remove dough from center of each cookie.** Fill cutout sections with crushed candy. If using cookies as hanging ornaments, make holes with a straw at top of cookies for string. Bake 7 to 9 minutes or until cookies are lightly browned and candy is melted. Slide foil off baking sheets. When cool, carefully loosen cookies from foil. If desired, decorate with frosting and other candies.
Makes about 2½ dozen medium cookies

*You will need a total measurement of about ⅓ cup crushed.

**Other shapes can be used to cut out center to make different designs.

Favorite recipe from The Sugar Association, Inc.

SPICY GINGERBREAD COOKIES

COOKIES
½ cup firmly packed brown sugar
¾ cup (1½ sticks) butter or
   margarine, softened
⅔ cup light molasses
1 egg
1½ teaspoons grated lemon peel
2½ cups all-purpose flour

1¼ teaspoons ground cinnamon
1 teaspoon vanilla
1 teaspoon ground allspice
½ teaspoon ground ginger
½ teaspoon baking soda
½ teaspoon salt
¼ teaspoon baking powder

FROSTING
4 cups confectioners' sugar
½ cup butter, softened
4 tablespoons milk

2 teaspoons vanilla
Food coloring (optional)

For Cookies, in large mixer bowl, combine brown sugar, ¾ cup butter, molasses, egg and lemon peel. Beat at medium speed, scraping bowl often, until smooth and creamy, 1 to 2 minutes. Add all remaining cookie ingredients. Reduce speed to low. Continue beating, scraping bowl often, until well mixed, 1 to 2 minutes. Cover; refrigerate at least 2 hours.

Preheat oven to 350°F. On well floured surface, roll out dough, one half at a time (keeping remaining dough refrigerated), to ¼-inch thickness. Cut with 3- to 4-inch cookie cutters. Place, 1 inch apart, on greased cookie sheets. Bake for 6 to 8 minutes or until no indentation remains when touched. Remove immediately. Cool completely.

For Frosting, in small mixer bowl combine confectioners' sugar, ½ cup butter, milk and 2 teaspoons vanilla. Beat at low speed, scraping bowl often, until fluffy, 1 to 2 minutes. If desired, color frosting with food coloring. Decorate cookies with frosting. *Makes about 4 dozen cookies*

Spicy Gingerbread Cookies

VERSATILE CUTOUT COOKIES

3½ cups unsifted flour
1 tablespoon baking powder
½ teaspoon salt
1 (14-ounce) can EAGLE® Brand
    Sweetened Condensed Milk (NOT
    evaporated milk)

¾ cup margarine or butter, softened
2 eggs
1 tablespoon vanilla extract *or* 2
    teaspoons almond or lemon
    extract

In small bowl, combine flour, baking powder and salt. In large mixer bowl, beat sweetened condensed milk, margarine, eggs and vanilla until well blended. Add dry ingredients; mix well. Cover; chill 2 hours.

Preheat oven to 350°F. On floured surface, knead dough to form a smooth ball. Divide into thirds. On well-floured surface, roll out each portion to ⅛-inch thickness. Cut with floured cookie cutter. Reroll as necessary to use all dough. Place, 1 inch apart, on greased cookie sheets. Bake 7 to 9 minutes or until lightly browned around edges (do not overbake). Cool. Frost and decorate as desired. Store loosely covered at room temperature.

Makes about 6½ dozen cookies

Versatile Cutout Cookies

Chocolate Cookies: Decrease flour to 3 cups. Add ½ cup HERSHEY⬝S Cocoa to dry ingredients. Chill and roll dough as directed. Makes about 6½ dozen cookies.

Sandwich Cookies: Prepare, chill and roll dough as directed. Use 2½-inch floured cookie cutter. Bake as directed. Sandwich two cookies together with ready-to-spread frosting. Sprinkle tops with confectioners' sugar, if desired. Makes about 3 dozen cookies.

Cookie Pecan Critters: Prepare and chill dough as directed. For each critter, arrange three pecan halves together on ungreased cookie sheets. Shape 1 teaspoonful dough into 1-inch ball. Press firmly onto center of arranged pecans. Repeat until all dough is used. Bake 12 to 14 minutes. Spread tops with Chocolate Frosting.* Makes about 6½ dozen cookies.

***Chocolate Frosting:** In small saucepan, melt ¼ cup margarine or butter with ¼ cup water. Stir in ½ cup HERSHEY⬝S Cocoa. Remove saucepan from heat; beat in 2 cups confectioners' sugar and 1 teaspoon vanilla until smooth. Stir in additional water for thinner consistency, if desired. Makes about 1 cup.

Mincemeat Peek-a-Boo Cookies: Prepare, chill and roll dough as directed. Use 3-inch floured round cookie cutter. Using sharp knife, cut "X" in center of half the rounds. Place 1 teaspoon mincemeat in center of remaining rounds. Top with cut rounds. Bake 8 to 10 minutes. Cool. Sprinkle with confectioners' sugar, if desired. Makes about 4 dozen cookies.

Stained Glass Cookies: Prepare, chill and roll dough as directed. Use 3-inch floured cookie cutter to cut into desired shapes. Cut out holes for "stained glass" in each cookie with small cutters or knife. Place on aluminum foil-lined cookie sheets. Fill holes with crushed hard candies. (If planning to hang cookies, make hole in each cookie in dough near edge with straw.) Bake 6 to 8 minutes or until candy has melted. Cool 10 minutes; remove from foil. Makes about 8 dozen cookies.

Cinnamon Pinwheel Cookies: Decrease baking powder to 2 teaspoons. Prepare and chill dough as directed. Divide into quarters. Roll each quarter of dough into a 16×8-inch rectangle. Brush with melted margarine or butter. Top each with 2 tablespoons sugar combined with ½ teaspoon ground cinnamon. Roll up tightly, beginning at 8-inch side. Wrap tightly; freeze until firm, about 20 minutes. Unwrap; cut into ¼-inch slices. Place on ungreased cookie sheets. Bake 12 to 14 minutes or until lightly browned. Makes about 6½ dozen cookies.

Chocolate Snow Balls: Prepare dough as directed for Chocolate Cookies, increasing eggs to three; add 1 cup finely chopped nuts. Chill. Shape into 1-inch balls. Roll in confectioners' sugar. Bake 8 to 10 minutes. Cool. Roll again in confectioners' sugar. Makes about 7½ dozen cookies.

Cookie Jar Classics

SPICY PUMPKIN COOKIES

2 cups CRISCO® All-Vegetable
    Shortening
2 cups sugar
1 can (16 ounces) solid-pack
    pumpkin
2 eggs
2 teaspoons vanilla
4 cups all-purpose flour

2 teaspoons baking powder
2 teaspoons cinnamon
1 teaspoon salt
1 teaspoon baking soda
1 teaspoon nutmeg
½ teaspoon allspice
2 cups raisins
1 cup chopped pecans or walnuts

1. Heat oven to 350°F. Grease baking sheets.

2. Combine shortening, sugar, pumpkin, eggs and vanilla in large bowl; beat well.

3. Combine flour, baking powder, cinnamon, salt, baking soda, nutmeg and allspice in large bowl. Add to batter; mix well. Stir in raisins and nuts.

4. Drop rounded teaspoonfuls of dough 2 inches apart onto greased baking sheets.

5. Bake at 350°F for 12 to 15 minutes. Cool 2 minutes on baking sheets. Remove to wire racks to cool completely.

Makes about 7 dozen cookies

Top to bottom: Drop Sugar Cookies (page 209); Spicy Pumpkin Cookies

SOFT SPICY MOLASSES COOKIES

2 cups all-purpose flour
1 cup sugar
¾ cup butter, softened
⅓ cup light molasses
3 tablespoons milk
1 egg

½ teaspoon baking soda
½ teaspoon ground ginger
½ teaspoon ground cinnamon
½ teaspoon ground cloves
⅛ teaspoon salt
Granulated sugar for rolling

In large mixer bowl, combine flour, 1 cup sugar, butter, molasses, milk, egg, baking soda, ginger, cinnamon, cloves and salt. Beat at low speed, scraping bowl often, until well mixed, 2 to 3 minutes. Cover; refrigerate until firm, at least 4 hours or overnight.

Preheat oven to 350°F. Shape rounded teaspoonfuls of dough into 1-inch balls. Roll in sugar. Place, 2 inches apart, on ungreased cookie sheets. Bake 10 to 12 minutes or until slightly firm to the touch. Remove immediately.

Makes about 4 dozen cookies

BUTTER–FLAVORED BRICKLE DRIZZLES

COOKIES
1¼ cups firmly packed light brown
    sugar
¾ cup BUTTER FLAVOR* CRISCO®
    All-Vegetable Shortening
1 egg
⅓ cup milk

1½ teaspoons vanilla
3 cups quick oats, uncooked
1 cup all-purpose flour
½ teaspoon baking soda
½ teaspoon salt
1 cup almond brickle chips

DRIZZLE
1 cup milk chocolate chips

1 teaspoon BUTTER FLAVOR*
    CRISCO® All-Vegetable
    Shortening

1. Heat oven to 375°F. Grease baking sheets.

2. **For cookies,** combine brown sugar, ¾ cup shortening, egg, milk and vanilla in large bowl. Beat at medium speed of electric mixer until well blended.

3. Combine oats, flour, baking soda and salt in small bowl. Mix into shortening mixture at low speed just until blended. Stir in almond brickle chips.

4. Shape dough into 1-inch balls. Place 2 inches apart on prepared baking sheets.

5. Bake at 375°F for 8 to 10 minutes or until lightly browned. Cool 2 minutes on baking sheets. Remove to wire racks to cool completely.

6. **For drizzle,** place chocolate chips and 1 teaspoon shortening in heavy resealable plastic food storage bag. Seal. Microwave at MEDIUM (50% power). Knead bag after 1 minute. Repeat until smooth. (Or, melt by placing in bowl of hot water.) Cut pinpoint hole in corner of bag. Squeeze out and drizzle over cookies.   *Makes about 6 dozen small cookies*

*BUTTER FLAVOR CRISCO® is artificially flavored.

Butter-Flavored Brickle Drizzles

Almond Milk Chocolate Chippers

ALMOND MILK CHOCOLATE CHIPPERS

1¼ cups all-purpose flour
½ teaspoon baking soda
½ teaspoon salt
½ cup butter or margarine, softened
½ cup packed light brown sugar
⅓ cup granulated sugar

1 large egg
2 tablespoons almond-flavored
  liqueur
1 cup milk chocolate chips
½ cup slivered almonds, toasted

Preheat oven to 375°F. In small bowl, combine flour, baking soda and salt; mix until well blended. Set aside. Beat butter, brown sugar and granulated sugar in large bowl until light and fluffy. Beat in egg until well blended. Beat in liqueur. Gradually add dry ingredients. Beat until well blended. Stir in chips and almonds. Drop dough by rounded teaspoonfuls, 2 inches apart, onto ungreased cookie sheets. Bake 9 to 10 minutes or until edges are golden brown. Let cookies stand on cookie sheets 2 minutes. Remove cookies with spatula to wire racks; cool completely. *Makes about 3 dozen cookies*

DROP SUGAR COOKIES

⅓ cup CRISCO® Oil
1 cup sugar
1 tablespoon vanilla
1 egg

2½ cups all-purpose flour
¾ teaspoon salt
½ teaspoon baking soda
¼ cup skim milk

1. Preheat oven to 400°F. Oil cookie sheet lightly.

2. Combine ⅓ cup Crisco® Oil, sugar and vanilla in large bowl. Add egg. Beat at medium speed of electric mixer until blended. Stir in flour, salt and baking soda with spoon. Stir until mixture is smooth. Add milk. Stir until well blended.

3. Drop dough by teaspoonfuls, 2 inches apart, onto cookie sheet. Flatten cookies with bottom of glass lightly oiled and dipped in sugar (or colored sugar).

4. Bake at 400°F for 6 to 8 minutes or until barely browned around edges. *Do not overbake.* Remove to cooling rack. *Makes about 3 dozen cookies*

IRRESISTIBLE PEANUT BUTTER COOKIES

1¼ cups firmly packed light brown
    sugar
¾ cup creamy peanut butter
½ cup CRISCO® All-Vegetable
    Shortening
3 tablespoons milk

1 tablespoon vanilla
1 egg
1¾ cups all-purpose flour
¾ teaspoon baking soda
¾ teaspoon salt

1. Heat oven to 375°F.

2. Combine brown sugar, peanut butter, shortening, milk and vanilla in large bowl. Beat at medium speed of electric mixer until well blended. Add egg. Beat just until blended.

3. Combine flour, baking soda and salt in small bowl. Add to shortening mixture at low speed. Mix just until blended.

4. Drop rounded teaspoonfuls of dough 2 inches apart onto ungreased baking sheets. Flatten slightly in crisscross pattern with floured fork tines.

5. Bake at 375°F for 7 to 8 minutes or until set and just beginning to brown. Cool 2 minutes on baking sheets. Remove to wire racks to cool completely. *Makes about 3 dozen cookies*

Clockwise from top: Chewy Oatmeal Cookies (page 212);
Irresistible Peanut Butter Cookies; Ultimate Chocolate Chip Cookies

ULTIMATE CHOCOLATE CHIP COOKIES

**1¼ cups firmly packed light brown
sugar
¾ cup BUTTER FLAVOR* CRISCO®
All-Vegetable Shortening
2 tablespoons milk
1 tablespoon vanilla**

**1 egg
1¾ cups all-purpose flour
1 teaspoon salt
¾ teaspoon baking soda
1 cup semisweet chocolate chips
1 cup coarsely chopped pecans****

1. Heat oven to 375°F.

2. Combine brown sugar, shortening, milk and vanilla in large bowl. Beat at medium speed of electric mixer until well blended. Beat egg into shortening mixture.

3. Combine flour, salt and baking soda in small bowl. Mix into shortening mixture at low speed just until blended. Stir in chocolate chips and nuts.

4. Drop rounded tablespoonfuls of dough 3 inches apart onto ungreased baking sheets.

5. Bake at 375°F for 8 to 10 minutes for chewy cookies or 11 to 13 minutes for crisp cookies. Cool 2 minutes on baking sheets. Remove to wire racks to cool completely.   *Makes about 3 dozen cookies*

*BUTTER FLAVOR CRISCO® is artificially flavored.

**You may substitute an additional ½ cup semisweet chocolate chips for the pecans.

Variations
Drizzle: Combine 1 teaspoon BUTTER FLAVOR* CRISCO® and 1 cup semisweet chocolate chips or 1 cup white melting chocolate, cut into small pieces, in microwave-safe measuring cup. Microwave at MEDIUM (50% power) 1 minute. Stir. Repeat until smooth. (Or, melt on rangetop in small saucepan over very low heat.) Drizzle back and forth over cookies. Sprinkle with nuts before chocolate hardens, if desired.

Chocolate Dipped: Melt chocolate as directed for Drizzle. Dip one end of each cooled cookie halfway into chocolate. Sprinkle with finely chopped nuts before chocolate hardens. Place on waxed paper until chocolate is firm.

CHEWY OATMEAL COOKIES

1¼ cups firmly packed light brown
    sugar
¾ cup BUTTER FLAVOR* CRISCO®
    All-Vegetable Shortening
1 egg
⅓ cup milk
1½ teaspoons vanilla

3 cups quick oats, uncooked
1 cup all-purpose flour
½ teaspoon baking soda
½ teaspoon salt
¼ teaspoon cinnamon
1 cup raisins
1 cup coarsely chopped walnuts

1. Heat oven to 375°F. Grease baking sheets.

2. Combine brown sugar, shortening, egg, milk and vanilla in large bowl. Beat at medium speed of electric mixer until well blended.

3. Combine oats, flour, baking soda, salt and cinnamon in medium bowl. Mix into shortening mixture at low speed just until blended. Stir in raisins and nuts.

4. Drop rounded tablespoonfuls of dough 2 inches apart onto prepared baking sheets.

5. Bake at 375°F for 10 to 12 minutes or until lightly browned. Cool 2 minutes on baking sheets. Remove to wire racks to cool completely.   *Makes about 2½ dozen cookies*

*BUTTER FLAVOR CRISCO® is artificially flavored.

PEANUT BUTTER REFRIGERATOR COOKIES

2½ cups flour
1 teaspoon baking powder
1 teaspoon baking soda
¼ teaspoon salt
1 cup MAZOLA® Margarine
1 cup SKIPPY® Creamy or Super
    Chunk® Peanut Butter

1 cup granulated sugar
1 cup packed brown sugar
2 eggs
1 teaspoon vanilla

In small bowl, combine flour, baking powder, baking soda and salt. In large bowl with mixer at medium speed, beat margarine and peanut butter until smooth. Beat in both sugars until blended. Beat in eggs and vanilla. Add flour mixture; beat until well blended. Shape dough into two rolls, 1½ inches in diameter. Wrap in plastic wrap; refrigerate until firm.

Preheat oven to 350°F. Slice rolls into ¼-inch-thick slices. Place, 2 inches apart, on ungreased cookie sheets. Bake 12 minutes or until lightly browned. Remove; cool completely on wire racks. Store in tightly covered container.   *Makes about 8 dozen cookies*

BUTTERSCOTCH FRUIT DROPS

2 cups all-purpose flour
1 teaspoon baking soda
½ teaspoon salt
½ cup (1 stick) butter or margarine,
   softened
¾ cup firmly packed brown sugar
1 egg
2 tablespoons milk

1 teaspoon grated lemon peel
   optional
2 cups (12-ounce package) NESTLÉ®
   Toll House® Butterscotch
   Flavored Morsels
1 cup diced mixed dried fruit bits or
   raisins

Preheat oven to 350°F. In small bowl, combine flour, baking soda and salt; set aside.

In large mixer bowl, beat butter and brown sugar until light and fluffy. Blend in egg, milk and lemon peel. Gradually beat in flour mixture. Stir in morsels and fruit. Drop by rounded measuring teaspoonfuls onto ungreased cookie sheets.

Bake 9 to 11 minutes until golden brown. Let stand 2 minutes. Remove from cookie sheets; cool on wire racks.
Makes about 6 dozen cookies

APPLESAUCE OATMEAL COOKIES

1 cup all-purpose flour
1 teaspoon baking powder
1 teaspoon ground allspice
1 teaspoon cinnamon
½ teaspoon nutmeg
½ teaspoon cloves
¼ teaspoon salt

½ cup margarine
½ cup packed brown sugar
2 egg whites
2 cups rolled oats
1 cup unsweetened applesauce
½ cup chopped raisins

Preheat oven to 375°F. Grease baking sheets. Mix flour, baking powder, spices and salt in small bowl. In large bowl, beat margarine and sugar until light and fluffy. Add egg whites; beat well. Add dry ingredients. Stir in oats, applesauce and raisins. Drop by level tablespoonfuls onto baking sheets. Bake 10 to 12 minutes or until edges are lightly browned. Cool on wire racks before serving.
Makes about 4 dozen cookies

Favorite recipe from Western New York Apple Growers Association, Inc.

SNICKERDOODLES

1½ cups granulated sugar, divided
1 cup BUTTER FLAVOR* CRISCO®
    All-Vegetable Shortening
2 eggs
¼ cup light corn syrup or regular
    pancake syrup

1 tablespoon vanilla
3 cups all-purpose flour
1½ teaspoons baking powder
½ teaspoon salt
1 teaspoon cinnamon

1. Heat oven to 400°F.

2. Combine 1¼ cups sugar and shortening in large bowl. Beat at medium speed of electric mixer until well blended. Add eggs, syrup and vanilla. Beat until light and fluffy.

3. Combine flour, baking powder and salt in large bowl. Gradually add to shortening mixture at low speed. Mix until well blended.

4. Shape into 1-inch balls. Combine remaining ¼ cup sugar and cinnamon in small bowl. Roll balls of dough in cinnamon-sugar mixture. Place 2 inches apart on ungreased baking sheets.

5. Bake at 400°F for 7 to 8 minutes. Remove to wire racks to cool completely.

Makes 6 to 7 dozen cookies

*BUTTER FLAVOR CRISCO® is artificially flavored.

PECAN CRUNCHIES

1 package DUNCAN HINES® Golden
    Sugar Cookie Mix
1 egg

1 tablespoon water
1½ cups crushed potato chips, divided
½ cup chopped pecans

1. Preheat oven to 375°F. Grease cookie sheets lightly.

2. Combine cookie mix, contents of buttery flavor packet from Mix, egg, water, ½ cup potato chips and pecans in large bowl. Stir until thoroughly blended. Form dough into 36 (1-inch) balls. Roll in remaining 1 cup crushed potato chips. Place, 2 inches apart, on cookie sheets. Flatten dough with fork.

3. Bake at 375°F for 8 to 10 minutes or until golden brown. Cool 1 minute on cookie sheets. Remove to cooling racks. Cool completely. Store in airtight container.

Makes about 3 dozen cookies

Top to bottom: Snickerdoodles; Pecan Crunchies

Brownie & Bar Greats

✿ ✿ ✿

APPLE CRUMB SQUARES

2 cups QUAKER® Oats (Quick or Old
    Fashioned), uncooked
1½ cups all-purpose flour
1 cup packed brown sugar
1 teaspoon ground cinnamon
½ teaspoon salt (optional)

½ teaspoon baking soda
¼ teaspoon ground nutmeg
¾ cup butter or margarine, melted
1 cup commercially prepared
    applesauce
½ cup chopped nuts

Preheat oven to 350°F. In large bowl, combine all ingredients except applesauce and nuts; mix until crumbly. Reserve 1 cup oats mixture. Press remaining oats mixture onto bottom of greased 13×9-inch pan. Bake 13 to 15 minutes; cool. Spread applesauce over partially baked crust; sprinkle with nuts. Sprinkle reserved 1 cup oats mixture over top. Bake 13 to 15 minutes or until golden brown. Cool in pan on wire racks; cut into 2-inch squares.

Makes about 24 squares

Apple Crumb Squares

FUDGY WALNUT COOKIE WEDGES

1 (20-ounce) package refrigerated
  cookie dough, any flavor
1 (12-ounce) package semisweet
  chocolate chips
2 tablespoons margarine or butter

1 (14-ounce) can EAGLE® Brand
  Sweetened Condensed Milk (NOT
  evaporated milk)
1 teaspoon vanilla extract
½ cup chopped walnuts

Preheat oven to 350°F. Divide cookie dough into thirds. With floured hands, press onto bottom of three aluminum foil-lined 9-inch round cake pans or press into 9-inch circles on ungreased baking sheets. Bake 10 to 20 minutes or until golden. Cool. In heavy saucepan, over medium heat, melt chips and margarine with sweetened condensed milk. Cook and stir until thickened, about 5 minutes; add vanilla. Spread over cookie circles. Top with walnuts. Chill. Cut into wedges. Store loosely covered at room temperature.   *Makes about 36 wedges*

Fudgy Walnut Cookie Wedges

PUMPKIN JINGLE BARS

¾ cup MIRACLE WHIP® Salad
  Dressing
1 two-layer spice cake mix
1 (16-ounce) can pumpkin
3 eggs

Confectioners' sugar
Vanilla frosting
Red and green gum drops, sliced

Preheat oven to 350°F. Mix salad dressing, cake mix, pumpkin and eggs in large bowl at medium speed of electric mixer until well blended. Pour into greased 15½×10½-inch jelly-roll pan. Bake 18 to 20 minutes or until edges pull away from sides of pan. Cool. Sprinkle with confectioners' sugar. Cut into bars. Decorate with frosting and gum drops.   *Makes about 36 bars*

Preparation time: 5 minutes
Baking time: 20 minutes

LEMON CRUNCHIES

1 (14- or 15-ounce) can sweetened
  condensed milk
½ cup lemon juice
1 teaspoon grated lemon peel
2 to 3 drops yellow food coloring
1½ cups sifted all-purpose flour
1 teaspoon DAVIS® Baking Powder

1 teaspoon salt
⅔ cup BLUE BONNET® Margarine,
  softened
1 cup firmly packed light brown
  sugar
1 cup quick-cooking oats

Blend sweetened condensed milk, juice, lemon peel and food coloring in medium bowl; set aside.

Sift together flour, baking powder and salt in small bowl. In large bowl with electric mixer, beat margarine and sugar until light and fluffy; mix in flour mixture and oats until crumbly.

Pat half the oat mixture onto bottom of well greased 8×8-inch pan. Spread milk mixture over crust; sprinkle with remaining oat mixture. Bake 30 minutes or until browned around pan edges. Cool in pan on wire rack for about 15 minutes; cut into bars. Chill until firm.   *Makes about 24 bars*

ULTIMATE DESIGNER BROWNIES

¾ cup HERSHEY®S Cocoa
½ teaspoon baking soda
⅔ cup butter or margarine, melted
    and divided
½ cup boiling water
2 cups sugar
2 eggs
1⅓ cups all-purpose flour
1 teaspoon vanilla extract

¼ teaspoon salt
¾ cup (3½-ounce jar) macadamia
    nuts, coarsely chopped
2 cups (12-ounce package)
    HERSHEY®S Semi-Sweet Chocolate
    Chips, divided
Vanilla Glaze (recipe follows)
½ teaspoon shortening (not butter,
    margarine or oil)

Preheat oven to 350°F. Grease 13×9-inch baking pan or two 8-inch square baking pans. In medium bowl, stir together cocoa and baking soda; blend in ⅓ cup melted butter. Add boiling water; stir until mixture thickens. Stir in sugar, eggs and remaining ⅓ cup melted butter; stir until smooth. Add flour, vanilla and salt; blend well. Stir in nuts and 1½ cups chocolate chips. Pour into prepared pan(s). Bake 30 to 35 minutes for square pans or 35 to 40 minutes for rectangular pan or until brownie begins to pull away from sides of pan. Cool completely in pan on wire rack.

Prepare Vanilla Glaze; spread glaze on top of brownies. Cut brownies into triangles. Place remaining ½ cup chips and shortening in top of double boiler over hot, not boiling, water; stir until melted. Put into pastry bag fitted with small writing tip. Pipe design on each brownie.   *Makes about 24 brownies*

VANILLA GLAZE

2 tablespoons butter or margarine
4 teaspoons milk
¼ teaspoon brandy extract

¼ teaspoon rum extract
1 cup powdered sugar

In small saucepan over low heat, melt butter in milk. Remove from heat; add brandy and rum extracts. Gradually add powdered sugar; beat with wire whisk until smooth. Makes about ½ cup glaze.

Streusel Caramel Bars

STREUSEL CARAMEL BARS

2 cups unsifted flour
¾ cup firmly packed light brown
    sugar
1 egg, beaten
¾ cup cold margarine or butter,
    divided

¾ cup chopped nuts
24 EAGLE™ Brand Caramels,
    unwrapped
1 (14-ounce) can EAGLE® Brand
    Sweetened Condensed Milk
    (NOT evaporated milk)

Preheat oven to 350°F. In large bowl, combine flour, sugar and egg; cut in *½ cup* margarine until crumbly. Stir in nuts. Reserving 2 cups crumb mixture, press remainder firmly onto bottom of greased 13×9-inch baking pan. Bake 15 minutes. Meanwhile, in heavy saucepan, over low heat, melt caramels with sweetened condensed milk and remaining *¼ cup* margarine. Pour over prepared crust. Top with reserved crumb mixture. Bake 20 minutes or until bubbly. Cool. Cut into bars. Store loosely covered at room temperature.

Makes 24 to 36 bars

Chocolate Caramel Bars: Melt 2 (1-ounce) squares unsweetened chocolate with caramels, sweetened condensed milk and margarine. Proceed as above.

Chocolate Caramel-Pecan Bars

CHOCOLATE CARAMEL-PECAN BARS

2 cups butter, softened, divided	⅔ cup packed light brown sugar
½ cup granulated sugar	¼ cup light corn syrup
1 large egg	2½ cups coarsely chopped pecans
2¾ cups all-purpose flour	1 cup semisweet chocolate chips

Preheat oven to 375°F. Grease 15×10-inch jelly-roll pan; set aside. Beat 1 cup butter and granulated sugar in large bowl until light and fluffy. Beat in egg. Add flour. Beat until well combined. Spread dough with rubber spatula into prepared pan. Bake 20 minutes or until light golden brown.

While bars are baking, combine remaining 1 cup butter, brown sugar and corn syrup in medium, heavy saucepan. Cook over medium heat until mixture boils, stirring frequently. Boil gently 2 minutes, without stirring. Quickly stir in pecans; spread evenly over base. Return to oven. Bake 20 minutes or until dark golden brown and bubbling. Immediately sprinkle chocolate chips evenly over hot caramel. Gently press chips into caramel topping with spatula. Loosen caramel from edges of pan with thin spatula or knife. Place pan on wire rack; cool completely. Cut into 3×1½-inch bars. *Makes about 40 bars*

BUTTERSCOTCH BROWNIES

2 cups all-purpose flour	½ cup (1 stick) butter
2 teaspoons baking powder	1 cup firmly packed brown sugar
1½ teaspoons salt	4 eggs
2 cups (12-ounce package) NESTLÉ®	1 teaspoon vanilla extract
Toll House® Butterscotch	1 cup chopped nuts
Flavored Morsels	

Preheat oven to 350°F. In small bowl, combine flour, baking powder and salt; set aside. Combine morsels and butter over hot, not boiling, water. Stir until morsels are melted and mixture is smooth. Transfer to large mixer bowl. Stir in brown sugar; cool 5 minutes. Beat in eggs and vanilla extract. Blend in flour mixture. Stir in nuts. Spread in greased 15½×10½-inch baking pan.

Bake 20 minutes. Cool. Cut into 2-inch squares. *Makes about 35 brownies*

PINEAPPLE ALMOND SHORTBREAD BARS

CRUST
1½ cups all-purpose flour
½ cup DOLE® Almonds, toasted,
   ground

¼ cup sugar
½ cup cold margarine

TOPPING
1 can (20 ounces) DOLE® Crushed
   Pineapple, drained
3 eggs
¼ cup sugar

¼ cup honey
1 tablespoon grated lemon peel
1½ cups DOLE® Slivered Almonds,
   toasted

For Crust, preheat oven to 350°F. In large bowl, combine flour, ground almonds and ¼ cup sugar. Cut in margarine until crumbly. Form dough into a ball; press into ungreased 13×9-inch baking pan. Bake 10 minutes. Cool slightly.

For Topping, in medium bowl, combine pineapple, eggs, ¼ cup sugar, honey and lemon peel. Stir in toasted almonds. Pour topping over partially baked crust. Bake an additional 30 to 35 minutes. Cool completely in pan on wire rack. Cut into bars.
Makes about 2 dozen bars

APPLE MACADAMIA NUT BARS

3 Golden Delicious apples, coarsely
   chopped
1 tablespoon lemon juice
1 (16-ounce) package pound cake
   mix
1 cup milk
1 teaspoon grated lemon peel

½ teaspoon almond extract
1 cup flaked, sweetened coconut
3½ ounces macadamia nuts, coarsely
   chopped
3½ ounces white chocolate, coarsely
   chopped

1. Heat oven to 350°F. Grease and flour 13×9-inch baking pan. Combine apples and lemon juice; set aside.

2. In large bowl, with electric mixer, beat together pound cake mix, milk, lemon peel and almond extract. Stir in coconut, macadamia nuts, white chocolate and the reserved apples; mix well.

3. Spoon batter into prepared pan. Bake 50 to 55 minutes or until center springs back when gently pressed. Cool in pan 5 minutes; cut into bars.
Makes 12 bars

Favorite recipe from Washington Apple Commission

MAGIC COOKIE BARS

½ cup margarine or butter
1½ cups graham cracker crumbs
1 (14-ounce) can EAGLE® Brand
    Sweetened Condensed Milk (NOT
    evaporated milk)

1 (6-ounce) package semisweet
    chocolate chips
1 (3½-ounce) can flaked coconut
    (1½ cups)
1 cup chopped nuts

Preheat oven to 350°F (325°F for glass dish). In 13×9-inch baking pan, melt margarine in oven. Sprinkle crumbs over margarine; pour sweetened condensed milk evenly over crumbs. Top with remaining ingredients; press down firmly. Bake 25 to 30 minutes or until lightly browned. Cool. Chill, if desired. Cut into bars. Store loosely covered at room temperature.   *Makes 24 to 36 bars*

Seven Layer Magic Cookie Bars: Add 1 (6-ounce) package butterscotch flavored chips after chocolate chips.

Magic Peanut Cookie Bars: Omit chocolate chips and chopped nuts. Top sweetened condensed milk with 2 cups (about ¾ pound) chocolate-covered peanuts, then coconut. Proceed as above.

Magic Cookie Bars

CHOCOLATE SCOTCHEROOS

1 cup light corn syrup
1 cup sugar
1 cup peanut butter
6 cups KELLOGG'S® RICE KRISPIES®
   Cereal

Vegetable cooking spray
1 package (6 ounces, 1 cup)
   semisweet chocolate morsels
1 package (6 ounces, 1 cup)
   butterscotch morsels

1. Measure corn syrup and sugar into large saucepan. Cook over medium heat, stirring frequently, until sugar dissolves and mixture begins to boil. Remove from heat. Stir in peanut butter. Mix well. Add Kellogg's® Rice Krispies® Cereal. Stir until well coated. Press mixture into 13×9-inch pan coated with cooking spray. Set aside.

2. Melt chocolate and butterscotch morsels together in small saucepan over low heat, stirring constantly. Spread evenly over cereal mixture. Let stand until firm. Cut into 2×1-inch bars to serve.

Makes about 48 bars

CHOCOLATE CHUNK BLONDE BROWNIES

½ cup (1 stick) margarine or butter,
   softened
1 cup firmly packed brown sugar
1 cup granulated sugar
4 eggs
2 teaspoons vanilla
2 cups all-purpose flour

1 teaspoon CALUMET® Baking
   Powder
¼ teaspoon salt
1 package (8 ounces) BAKER'S®
   Semi-Sweet Chocolate, coarsely
   chopped
1 cup chopped nuts

Preheat oven to 350°F.

Beat margarine, both sugars, eggs and vanilla in large bowl until light and fluffy. Mix in flour, baking powder and salt until well blended. Stir in chocolate and nuts. Spread into greased 13×9-inch pan.

Bake for 30 minutes or until toothpick inserted into center comes out with moist crumbs. Do not overbake. Cool in pan; cut into squares.

Makes about 24 brownies

Prep time: 20 minutes
Baking time: 30 minutes

Chocolate Scotcheroos

Top to bottom: Peachy Oatmeal Bars; Streusel Strawberry Bars

PEACHY OATMEAL BARS

CRUMB MIXTURE
1½ cups all-purpose flour
1 cup quick-cooking oats
½ cup sugar
½ teaspoon baking soda

¼ teaspoon salt
¾ cup margarine, melted
2 teaspoons almond extract

FILLING
¾ cup peach or apricot preserves

⅓ cup flaked coconut

Preheat oven to 350°F.

For Crumb Mixture, combine all crumb mixture ingredients in large mixer bowl. Beat at low speed, scraping bowl often, until mixture is crumbly, 1 to 2 minutes. *Reserve ¾ cup crumb mixture;* press remaining crumb mixture onto bottom of greased 9-inch square baking pan.

For Filling, spread preserves to within ½ inch of edge of crust; sprinkle with reserved crumb mixture and coconut. Bake for 20 to 25 minutes or until edges are lightly browned. Cool completely. Cut into bars.
Makes about 24 bars

STREUSEL STRAWBERRY BARS

1 cup butter or margarine, softened
1 cup sugar
1 egg
2 cups all-purpose flour

¾ cup pecans, coarsely chopped
1 jar (10 ounces) strawberry or
    raspberry preserves

Preheat oven to 350°F. Combine butter and sugar in large mixer bowl. Beat at low speed, scraping bowl often, until well blended. Add egg and flour. Beat until mixture is crumbly, 2 to 3 minutes. Stir in pecans. Reserve 1 cup crumb mixture; press remaining crumb mixture onto bottom of greased 9-inch square baking pan. Spread preserves to within ½ inch of edge of crust. Crumble reserved crumb mixture over preserves. Bake for 40 to 50 minutes or until lightly browned. Cool completely. Cut into bars.
Makes about 24 bars

CRANBERRY JEWEL BARS

2 cups unsifted flour
1½ cups quick-cooking or
   old-fashioned oats
¾ cup plus 1 tablespoon firmly
   packed brown sugar
1 cup *cold* margarine or butter
1 (14-ounce) can EAGLE® Brand
   Sweetened Condensed Milk (NOT
   evaporated milk)

1 cup ricotta cheese
2 eggs
1½ teaspoons vanilla extract
1 teaspoon grated orange peel
2 tablespoons cornstarch
1 (16-ounce) can whole berry
   cranberry sauce

Preheat oven to 350°F. In large bowl, combine flour, oats and ¾ *cup* brown sugar. Cut in *cold* margarine until crumbly. Reserving 2 cups crumb mixture, press remainder firmly onto bottom of 13×9-inch baking pan. Bake 15 minutes.

Meanwhile, in small mixer bowl, beat sweetened condensed milk, ricotta cheese, eggs, vanilla and orange peel until smooth. Spread evenly over baked crust. In small bowl, combine remaining *1 tablespoon* sugar and cornstarch; stir in cranberry sauce. Spoon over cheese layer. Top with reserved crumb mixture. Bake 40 minutes or until lightly browned. Cool. Chill. Garnish as desired. Cut into bars. Store covered in refrigerator.   *Makes 36 to 40 bars*

EXTRA MOIST & CHUNKY BROWNIES

1 (8-ounce) package cream cheese,
   softened
1 cup sugar
1 egg
1 teaspoon vanilla extract
¾ cup all-purpose flour

1 (3⅜-ounce) package ROYAL®
   Chocolate or Dark 'N' Sweet
   Chocolate Pudding & Pie Filling
4 (1-ounce) semisweet chocolate
   squares, chopped

In large bowl, with electric mixer at high speed, beat cream cheese, sugar, egg and vanilla until smooth; blend in flour and pudding mix. Spread batter into greased 8×8-inch microwavable dish; sprinkle with chocolate. Shield corners of dish with waxed paper. Microwave at HIGH (100% power) for 8 to 10 minutes or until toothpick inserted in center comes out clean, rotating dish 90° turn every 2 minutes. Cool completely in pan. Cut into squares.   *Makes about 16 brownies*

MINTED CHOCOLATE CHIP BROWNIES

¾ cup granulated sugar
½ cup butter or margarine
2 tablespoons water
1 cup semisweet chocolate chips or
    mini chocolate chips
1½ teaspoons vanilla

2 large eggs
1¼ cups all-purpose flour
½ teaspoon baking soda
½ teaspoon salt
1 cup mint chocolate chips
Confectioners' sugar for garnish

Preheat oven to 350°F. Combine granulated sugar, butter and water in medium microwavable bowl. Microwave on HIGH (100% power) 2½ to 3 minutes or until butter is melted. Stir in semisweet chips; stir gently until chips are melted and mixture is well blended. Stir in vanilla; let stand 5 minutes to cool. Beat eggs into chocolate mixture, one at a time. Combine flour, baking soda and salt in small bowl. Add to chocolate mixture. Stir in mint chips. Spread into greased 9-inch square baking pan.

Bake 25 minutes for fudgy brownies or 30 to 35 minutes for cake-like brownies. Remove pan to wire rack; cool completely. Cut into 2¼-inch squares. Sprinkle with confectioners' sugar, if desired.

Makes 16 brownies

Minted Chocolate Chip Brownies

Acknowledgments

Almond Board of California

American Dairy Industry Association

American Egg Board

Best Foods, a Division of CPC International

Blue Diamond Growers

Borden Kitchens, Borden, Inc.

California Apricot Advisory Board

Checkerboard Kitchens, Ralston Purina Company

Diamond Walnut Growers, Inc.

Dole Food Company, Inc.

Domino Sugar Corporation

Filippo Berio Olive Oil

Florida Department of Citrus

Hershey Chocolate U.S.A.

Kahlúa Liqueur

Kellogg Company

Kraft General Foods, Inc.

Leaf®, Inc.

M & M/Mars

Nabisco Foods Group

Nestlé Food Company

The Procter & Gamble Company

The Quaker Oats Company

Sokol and Company

The Sugar Association, Inc.

Sun • Maid Growers of California

USA Rice Council

Walnut Marketing Board

Washington Apple Commission

Western New York Apple Growers Association, Inc.

Wisconsin Milk Marketing Board

Photo Credits

Almond Board of California

American Dairy Industry Association

Best Foods, a Division of CPC International

Borden Kitchens, Borden, Inc.

California Apricot Advisory Board

Dole Food Company, Inc.

Hershey Chocolate U.S.A.

Kraft General Foods, Inc.

Leaf ®, Inc.

Nestlé Food Company

The Procter & Gamble Company

The Quaker Oats Company

Sokol and Company

USA Rice Council

Walnut Marketing Board

Wisconsin Milk Marketing Board

Index

A

All-American Chocolate Chip Cookies, 106
Almond Apricot Bars, 56
Almond Cream Cookies, 162
Almond Double Chip Cookies, 101
Almond Dream Bars, 59
Almond Frosting, 33
Almond Icing, 59
Almond Melting Moments, 178
Almond Milk Chocolate Chippers, 209
Almond Raspberry Macaroons, 17
Almond-Raspberry Thumbprint Cookies, 157
Almond Rice Madeleines, 70
Almond Toffee Triangles, 50
Anise Pillows, 94
Anise Stars, 167
Apple Crumb Squares, 216
Apple Macadamia Nut Bars, 224
Applesauce Fruitcake Bars, 58
Applesauce Oatmeal Cookies, 213
Apricot-Pecan Tassies, 14
Auntie Van's Christmas Cookies, 124
Austrian Tea Cookies, 187

B

Baked S'Mores, 135
Banana Bars, 137
Banana-Date Bars, 59
Banana Gingerbread Bars, 144
Bar Cookie Crust, 63
Bar Cookies
 Almond Apricot Bars, 56
 Almond Dream Bars, 59
 Almond Toffee Triangles, 50
 Apple Crumb Squares, 216
 Apple Macadamia Nut Bars, 224
 Applesauce Fruitcake Bars, 58
 Baked S'Mores, 135
 Banana Bars, 137
 Banana-Date Bars, 59
 Banana Gingerbread Bars, 144
 Black Russian Brownies, 135

Bar Cookies, *continued*
 Blonde Brickle Brownies, 60
 Butterscotch Brownies, 223
 Chocolate Apple Crisp, 140
 Chocolate Caramel Bars, 221
 Chocolate Caramel-Pecan Bars, 223
 Chocolate Cherry Brownies, 54
 Chocolate Chunk Blonde Brownies, 226
 Chocolate Cream Cheese Sugar Cookie Bars, 113
 Chocolate-Drizzled Peanut Bars, 62
 Chocolate-Frosted Almond Bars, 167
 Chocolate Peanut Butter Squares, 65
 Chocolate Pecan Pie Bars, 63
 Chocolate Scotcheroos, 226
 Cranberry Jewel Bars, 230
 Cranberry Walnut Bars, 64
 Crispy Nut Shortbread, 21
 Deluxe Toll House® Mud Bars, 51
 English Toffee Bars, 52
 Extra Moist & Chunky Brownies, 230
 Fancy Walnut Brownies, 77
 Frosted Toffee Bars, 141
 Fruit and Chocolate Dream Squares, 136
 Fudgy Walnut Cookie Wedges, 218
 Hershey®s Chocolate Chip Blondies, 20
 Hershey®s Premium Double Chocolate Brownies, 60
 Holiday Chocolate Chip Cookies, 27
 Kahlúa® Mudslide Brownies, 109
 Lemon Crunchies, 219
 Linzer Bars, 55
 Magic Cookie Bars, 225
 Mallow-Graham Bars, 145
 Mint Chocolate Truffle Bars, 64
 Minted Chocolate Chip Brownies, 231
 Mocha Brownies, 141
 Oatmeal Extravaganzas, 145
 One Bowl Brownies, 132
 Orange Pumpkin Bars, 55
 Peachy Oatmeal Bars, 229
 Peanut Butter Bars, 52
 Peanut Butter Chocolate Bars, 20

Bar Cookies, *continued*
 Peanut Butter Raisin Bars, 136
 Peanut Butter Swirl Brownies, 134
 Pecan Caramel Bars, 51
 Pecan Date Bars, 48
 Pecan Mince Bars, 54
 Pecan Turtle Bars, 134
 Pineapple Almond Shortbread Bars, 224
 Pineapple Pecan Bars, 139
 Pumpkin Jingle Bars, 219
 Pumpkin Pecan Pie Bars, 57
 Raspberry Meringue Bars, 139
 Rich 'n' Creamy Brownie Bars, 142
 Rocky Road Brownies, 134
 Spiced Mincemeat Squares, 142
 Streusel Caramel Bars, 221
 Streusel Strawberry Bars, 229
 Ultimate Designer Brownies, 220
Bavarian Cookie Wreaths, 19
Bittersweet Glaze, 69
Black Russian Brownies, 135
Blonde Brickle Brownies, 60
Brandy Lace Cookies, 66
Brownie Cookie Bites, 47
Butter Cookies, 192
Butter-Flavored Brickle Drizzles, 206
Butterscotch Brownies, 223
Butterscotch Fruit Drops, 213

C

Candy Shop Pizza, 154
Caramel Filling, 79
Caramel Lace Chocolate Chip Cookies, 81
Cherry Coconut Cookies, 184
Cherry Dot Cookies, 164
Cherry Rum Cookies, 174
Cherry Surprises, 150
Cherry Thumbprint Cookies, 172
Chewy Oatmeal Cookies, 212
Choco-Caramel Delights, 79
Choco-Cherry Cookies Supreme, 181
Choco-Coco Pecan Crisps, 10
Chocolate
 All-American Chocolate Chip Cookies, 106

Chocolate, *continued*

Almond Double Chip Cookies, 101
Almond Milk Chocolate Chippers, 209
Apple Macadamia Nut Bars, 224
Baked S'Mores, 135
Banana Bars, 137
Black Russian Brownies, 135
Brownie Cookie Bites, 47
Butter-Flavored Brickle Drizzles, 206
Candy Shop Pizza, 154
Caramel Lace Chocolate Chip Cookies, 81
Cherry Surprises, 150
Choco-Caramel Delights, 79
Choco-Cherry Cookies Supreme, 181
Chocolate Apple Crisp, 140
Chocolate Caramel Bars, 221
Chocolate Caramel-Pecan Bars, 223
Chocolate-Caramel Sugar Cookies, 102
Chocolate Cherry Brownies, 54
Chocolate Cherry Cookies, 40
Chocolate Chip & Mint Meringue Cookies, 179
Chocolate Chip Glaze, 30
Chocolate Chip Lollipops, 105
Chocolate Chips Thumbprint Cookies, 98
Chocolate Chunk Blonde Brownies, 226
Chocolate Cookies, 195
Chocolate-Dipped Almond Crescents, 80
Chocolate-Dipped Almond Horns, 16, 164
Chocolate-Dipped Brandy Snaps, 176
Chocolate-Dipped Oat Cookies, 79
Chocolate-Dipped Sugar Cookies, 38
Chocolate-Drizzled Peanut Bars, 62
Chocolate-Frosted Almond Bars, 167
Chocolate-Frosted Lebkuchen, 68
Chocolate-Gilded Danish Sugar Cones, 146
Chocolate Gingerbread Cookies, 198
Chocolate Kahlúa® Bears, 37
Chocolate Lace Cornucopias, 114
Chocolate Mint Pinwheels, 106
Chocolate Mint Snow-Top Cookies, 109
Chocolate Mint Sugar Cookie Drops, 112

Chocolate, *continued*

Chocolate Nut Slices, 46
Chocolate Nut Sugar Cookies, 38
Chocolate Peanut Butter Cups, 182
Chocolate Peanut Butter Squares, 65
Chocolate Pistachio Fingers, 72
Chocolate Raspberry Linzer Cookies, 108
Chocolate Scotcheroos, 226
Chocolate Spritz, 43
Chocolate Sugar Cookies, 102
Chocolate Thumbprints, 186
Confetti Cutouts, 34
Crispy Nut Shortbread, 21
Deluxe Toll House® Mud Bars, 51
Double-Dipped Hazelnut Crisps, 74
Double Surprise Cookies, 168
English Toffee Bars, 52
Extra Moist & Chunky Brownies, 230
Fancy Walnut Brownies, 77
Frosted Toffee Bars, 141
Fruit and Chocolate Dream Squares, 136
Fudgy Walnut Cookie Wedges, 218
Giant Oatmeal Cookies, 129
Hershey®s Chocolate Chip Blondies, 20
Hershey®s Premium Double Chocolate Brownies, 60
Hidden Treasures, 26
Holiday Chocolate Chip Cookies, 27
Holiday Fruit Drops, 12
Island Treasure Cookies, 25
Jam-Filled Chocolate Sugar Cookies, 102
Kahlúa® Mudslide Brownies, 109
Magic Cookie Bars, 225
"M&M's" Chocolate Candies Easy Party Cookies, 29
Milk Chocolate Florentine Cookies, 92
Mini Morsel Granola Cookies, 128
Mini Morsel Meringue Wreaths, 70
Mint Chocolate Chews, 105
Mint Chocolate Truffle Bars, 64
Minted Chocolate Chip Brownies, 231
Mocha Brownies, 141
New Wave Chocolate Spritz Cookies, 108
Nutty Chocolate Stars, 117
Oatmeal Extravaganzas, 145
One Bowl Brownies, 132

Chocolate, *continued*

Original Toll House® Chocolate Chip Cookies, 110
Peanut Butter Chocolate Bars, 20
Peanut Butter Jumbos, 101
Peanut Butter Pizza Cookies, 126
Peanut Butter Reindeer, 87
Peanut Butter Spritz Sandwiches, 118
Peanut Butter Stars, 171
Peanut Butter Sugar Cookies, 192
Peanut Butter Swirl Brownies, 134
Pecan Caramel Bars, 51
Pecan Florentines, 76
Pecan Turtle Bars, 134
Rocky Road Brownies, 134
Snow Caps, 148
Special Chocolate Chip Sandwiches, 156
Triple Chocolate Cookies, 44
Triple Chocolate Pretzels, 42
Ultimate Chocolate Chip Cookies, 211
Ultimate Designer Brownies, 220
White Brownie Bites, 69
White Chocolate Biggies, 100
Chocolate Cookies, 202
Chocolate Filling, 29
Chocolate Frosting, 44, 203
Chocolate Glaze, 18, 62, 191
Chocolate Icing, 37
Chocolate Madeleines, 44
Chocolate Melting Moments, 113
Chocolate Pecan Pie Bars, 63
Christmas Stained Glass Cookies, 199
Christmas Treasure Nuggets, 95
Chunky Butter Christmas Cookies, 121
Cinnamon Pinwheel Cookies, 203
Cinnamon Stars, 190
Cocoa
Choco-Caramel Delights, 79
Choco-Cherry Cookies Supreme, 181
Choco-Coco Pecan Crisps, 10
Chocolate Cookies, 202
Chocolate Cookie Sandwiches, 43
Chocolate Cream Cheese Sugar Cookie Bars, 113
Chocolate Frosting, 203
Chocolate Gingerbread Cookies, 198
Chocolate Madeleines, 44
Chocolate Melting Moments, 113
Chocolate Peanut Butter Cups, 182

Cocoa, *continued*
Chocolate Pecan Pie Bars, 63
Chocolate Snow Balls, 203
Chocolate Thumbprints, 186
Cocoa Almond Cutout Cookies, 191
Cocoa Gingerbread Cookies, 36
Hershey®s Premium Double Chocolate
  Brownies, 60
Mint Chocolate Truffle Bars, 64
Mocha Mint Crisps, 153
Peanut Butter and Chocolate Cookie
  Sandwich Cookies, 116
Pinecone Cookies, 157
Pinwheel Cookies, 76
Ultimate Designer Brownies, 220
White Chocolate Biggies, 100
Coffee Frosting, 125
Confectioners' Sugar Glaze, 129
Confetti Cutouts, 34
Cookie Glaze, 195
Cookie Pecan Critters, 203
Corn Flake Macaroons, 177
Cranberry Jewel Bars, 230
Cranberry Walnut Bars, 64
Cream Cheese Cookies, 184
Cream Cheese Cutout Cookies, 33
Cream Cheese Pastry, 73
Creamy Coffee Frosting, 141
Creamy Vanilla Frosting, 38
Creme Filling, 43
Crispy Nut Shortbread, 21
Cutout Cookies
Anise Stars, 67
Auntie Van's Christmas Cookies, 124
Austrian Tea Cookies, 187
Butter Cookies, 192
Chocolate Cookies, 195, 202
Chocolate Gingerbread Cookies, 198
Chocolate Kahlúa® Bears, 37
Chocolate Raspberry Linzer Cookies,
  108
Christmas Stained Glass Cookies, 199
Cinnamon Stars, 190
Cocoa Almond Cutout Cookies, 191
Cocoa Gingerbread Cookies, 36
Confetti Cutouts, 34
Cream Cheese Cutout Cookies, 33
Cutout Sugar Cookies, 38
Double-Dipped Hazelnut Crisps, 74
Dutch St. Nicholas Cookies, 37

Cutout Cookies, *continued*
European Kolacky, 13
Frosted Butter Cookies, 188
Gingerbread Cookies, 152
Glazed Sugar Cookies, 84
Hanukkah Cookies, 196
Holiday Gingerbread People, 190
Holiday Shortbread with Variations, 167
Kittens and Mittens, 194
Lemon Cutout Cookies, 34
Linzer Tarts, 88
Mincemeat Peek-a-Boo Cookies, 203
Peanut Butter Cutout Cookies, 30
Peanut Butter Gingerbread Men, 36
Peanut Butter Reindeer, 87
Peanut Butter Sugar Cookies, 192
Pinecone Cookies, 157
Spicy Gingerbread Cookies, 200
Stained Glass Cookies, 97, 203
Sugar Cookies, 89
Versatile Cutout Cookies, 202
Cutout Sugar Cookies, 38

D
Date-Nut Macaroons, 173
Decorator Icing, 36
Deluxe Toll House® Mud Bars, 51
Double Almond Butter Cookies, 25
Double Crunch Biscotti, 160
Double-Dipped Hazelnut Crisps, 74
Double Surprise Cookies, 168
Drop Cookies
All-American Chocolate Chip Cookies,
  106
Almond Cream Cookies, 162
Almond Double Chip Cookies, 101
Almond Milk Chocolate Chippers, 209
Almond Raspberry Macaroons, 17
Anise Pillows, 94
Applesauce Oatmeal Cookies, 213
Brownie Cookie Bites, 47
Butterscotch Fruit Drops, 213
Caramel Lace Chocolate Chip Cookies,
  81
Chewy Oatmeal Cookies, 212
Choco-Cherry Cookies Supreme, 181
Chocolate Chip & Mint Meringue
  Cookies, 179
Chocolate-Frosted Lebkuchen, 68
Christmas Treasure Nuggets, 95

Drop Cookies, *continued*
Chunky Butter Christmas Cookies, 121
Corn Flake Macaroons, 177
Cream Cheese Cookies, 184
Date-Nut Macaroons, 173
Drop Sugar Cookies, 209
Florentine Cups, 152
Holiday Fruit Drops, 12
Irresistible Peanut Butter Cookies, 210
Island Treasure Cookies, 25
"M&M's" Chocolate Candies Easy Party
  Cookies, 29
Marvelous Macaroons, 131
Merry Cherry Macaroons, 24
Milk Chocolate Florentine Cookies, 92
Mini Morsel Granola Cookies, 128
Mint Chocolate Chews, 105
Oatmeal-Banana Lebkuchen, 94
Oatmeal Cranberry-Nut Cookies, 149
Oatmeal Scotchies, 122
Orange Pecan Gems, 149
Original Toll House® Chocolate Chip
  Cookies, 110
Peanut Butter Jumbos, 101
Pecan Florentines, 76
Peppermint Macaroons, 168
Pineapple-Oatmeal Cookies, 124
Pineapple-Raisin Jumbles, 120
Snow Caps, 148
Spicy Pumpkin Cookies, 204
Triple Chocolate Cookies, 44
Ultimate Chocolate Chip Cookies, 211
White Brownie Bites, 69
White Chocolate Biggies, 100
Dutch St. Nicholas Cookies, 37

E
English Toffee Bars, 52
European Kolacky, 13
Extra Moist & Chunky Brownies, 230

F
Fancy Walnut Brownies, 77
Favorite Peanut Butter Cookies, 131
Florentine Cups, 152
Frosted Butter Cookies, 188
Frosted Toffee Bars, 141
Frosty Cherry Cookies, 163
Fruit and Chocolate Dream Squares, 136
Fudgy Walnut Cookie Wedges, 218

G
Giant Oatmeal Cookies, 129
Gingerbread Cookies, 152
Glazed Sugar Cookies, 84

H
Hanukkah Cookies, 196
Hershey‚s Chocolate Chip Blondies, 20
Hershey‚s Premium Double Chocolate Brownies, 60
Hidden Treasures, 26
Holiday Almond Wreaths, 89
Holiday Chocolate Chip Cookies, 27
Holiday Citrus Logs, 23
Holiday Fruit Drops, 12
Holiday Gingerbread People, 190
Holiday Shortbread with Variations, 167
Holiday Teatime Treats, 153
Honey-Ginger Bourbon Balls, 12

I
Irresistible Peanut Butter Cookies, 210
Island Treasure Cookies, 25

J
Jam-Filled Chocolate Sugar Cookies, 102
Jingle Jumbles, 22

K
Kahlúa® Glaze, 109
Kahlúa® Mudslide Brownies, 109
Kentucky Bourbon Pecan Tarts, 73
Kittens and Mittens, 194
Kolacky, 169

L
Lemon Blossom Cookies, 13
Lemon Crunchies, 219
Lemon Cutout Cookies, 34
Lemon Glaze, 95
Lemon Icing, 35
Lemon Pecan Crescents, 173
Lemon Wafers, 24
Lemony Spritz Sticks, 18
Linzer Bars, 55
Linzer Tarts, 88

M
Magic Cookie Bars, 225
Mallow-Graham Bars, 145

"M&M's" Chocolate Candies Easy Party Cookies, 29
Marvelous Macaroons, 131
Melting Moments, 178
Meringue Topping, 139
Merry Cherry Macaroons, 24
Milk Chocolate Florentine Cookies, 92
Mincemeat Peek-a-Boo Cookies, 203
Mini Morsel Granola Cookies, 128
Mini Morsel Meringue Wreaths, 70
Mint Chocolate Chews, 105
Mint Chocolate Truffle Bars, 64
Minted Chocolate Chip Brownies, 231
Mocha Brownies, 141
Mocha Filling, 113
Mocha Glaze, 42
Mocha Mint Crisps, 153
Mocha Mint Sugar, 153

N
New Wave Chocolate Spritz Cookies, 108
No-Bake Cookies
  Holiday Citrus Logs, 23
  Honey-Ginger Bourbon Balls, 12
  No-Bake Peanutty Cookies, 178
Noel Tarts, 167
Norwegian Molasses Cookies, 129
Nuts
  All-American Chocolate Chip Cookies, 106
  Almond Apricot Bars, 56
  Almond Cream Cookies, 162
  Almond Double Chip Cookies, 101
  Almond Dream Bars, 59
  Almond Melting Moments, 178
  Almond Milk Chocolate Chippers, 209
  Almond Rice Madeleines, 70
  Almond Toffee Triangles, 50
  Anise Pillows, 94
  Apple Crumb Squares, 216
  Apple Macadamia Nut Bars, 224
  Applesauce Fruitcake Bars, 58
  Apricot-Pecan Tassies, 14
  Banana-Date Bars, 59
  Banana Gingerbread Bars, 144
  Black Russian Brownies, 135
  Butterscotch Brownies, 223
  Caramel Lace Chocolate Chip Cookies, 81

Nuts, *continued*
  Cherry Coconut Cookies, 184
  Cherry Dot Cookies, 164
  Cherry Thumbprint Cookies, 172
  Chewy Oatmeal Cookies, 212
  Choco-Caramel Delights, 79
  Choco-Coco Pecan Crisps, 10
  Chocolate Apple Crisp, 140
  Chocolate Caramel-Pecan Bars, 223
  Chocolate Chips Thumbprint Cookies, 98
  Chocolate Chunk Blonde Brownies, 226
  Chocolate-Dipped Almond Horns, 16, 164
  Chocolate-Dipped Oat Cookies, 79
  Chocolate-Drizzled Peanut Bars, 62
  Chocolate-Frosted Almond Bars, 167
  Chocolate-Frosted Lebkuchen, 68
  Chocolate Lace Cornucopias, 114
  Chocolate Nut Slices, 46
  Chocolate Nut Sugar Cookies, 38
  Chocolate Peanut Butter Cups, 182
  Chocolate Pecan Pie Bars, 63
  Chocolate Pistachio Fingers, 72
  Chocolate Snow Balls, 203
  Chunky Butter Christmas Cookies, 121
  Cocoa Almond Cutout Cookies, 191
  Cookie Pecan Critters, 203
  Corn Flake Macaroons, 177
  Cranberry Walnut Bars, 64
  Cream Cheese Cookies, 184
  Crispy Nut Shortbread, 21
  Date-Nut Macaroons, 173
  Deluxe Toll House® Mud Bars, 51
  Double Almond Butter Cookies, 25
  Double-Dipped Hazelnut Crisps, 74
  Dutch St. Nicholas Cookies, 37
  English Toffee Bars, 52
  Fancy Walnut Brownies, 77
  Fruit and Chocolate Dream Squares, 136
  Fudgy Walnut Cookie Wedges, 218
  Giant Oatmeal Cookies, 129
  Holiday Almond Wreaths, 89
  Holiday Chocolate Chip Cookies, 27
  Holiday Citrus Logs, 23
  Holiday Fruit Drops, 12
  Honey-Ginger Bourbon Balls, 12

Nuts, *continued*
Island Treasure Cookies, 25
Kahlúa® Mudslide Brownies, 109
Kentucky Bourbon Pecan Tarts, 73
Lemon Pecan Cresents, 173
Linzer Bars, 55
Linzer Tarts, 88
Magic Cookie Bars, 225
Mallow-Graham Bars, 145
Marvelous Macaroons, 131
Mint Chocolate Chews, 105
Mocha Brownies, 141
Nutty Chocolate Stars, 117
Oatmeal-Banana Lebkuchen, 94
Oatmeal Cranberry-Nut Cookies, 149
Orange Pecan Gems, 149
Orange Pumpkin Bars, 55
Original Toll House® Chocolate Chip
    Cookies, 110
Peanut Butter Bars, 52
Peanut Butter Chocolate Bars, 20
Peanut Butter Cutout Cookies, 30
Pecan Caramel Bars, 51
Pecan Crunchies, 214
Pecan Date Bars, 48
Pecan Drops, 181
Pecan Florentines, 76
Pecan Mince Bars, 54
Pecan Turtle Bars, 134
Pineapple Almond Shortbread Bars, 224
Pineapple-Oatmeal Cookies, 124
Pineapple Pecan Bars, 139
Pineapple-Raisin Jumbles, 120
Pumpkin Pecan Pie Bars, 57
Raspberry Almond Sandwich Cookies,
    177
Raspberry Meringue Bars, 139
Rich 'n' Creamy Brownie Bars, 142
Rocky Road Brownies, 134
Santa's Thumbprints, 87
Sesame-Almond Cookies, 125
Snowballs, 14
Snow-Covered Almond Crescents, 90
Spicy Pumpkin Cookies, 204
Streusel Caramel Bars, 221
Streusel Strawberry Bars, 229
Toffee Tassies, 183
Triple Chocolate Cookies, 44
Ultimate Chocolate Chip Cookes, 211
Ultimate Designer Brownies, 220

Nuts, *continued*
Walnut Christmas Balls, 29
Walnut Jam Crescents, 186
White Chocolate Biggies, 100

O
Oatmeal-Banana Lebkuchen, 94
Oatmeal Cranberry-Nut Cookies, 149
Oatmeal Extravaganzas, 145
Oatmeal Scotchies, 122
Oats 'n' Pumpkin Pinwheels, 80
One Bowl Brownies, 132
Orange Pecan Gems, 149
Orange Pumpkin Bars, 55
Orange Sugar Cookies, 121
Original Toll House® Chocolate Chip
    Cookies, 110

P
Peachy Oatmeal Bars, 229
Peanut Butter
    Candy Shop Pizza, 154
    Chocolate Peanut Butter Cups, 182
    Chocolate Peanut Butter Squares, 65
    Chocolate Scotcheroos, 226
    Chocolate Thumbprints, 186
    Double Surprise Cookies, 168
    Favorite Peanut Butter Cookies, 131
    Irresistible Peanut Butter Cookies, 210
    No-Bake Peanutty Cookies, 178
    Peanut Butter Bars, 52
    Peanut Butter Chocolate Bars, 20
    Peanut Butter Cookies, 122
    Peanut Butter Crackles, 22
    Peanut Butter Cutout Cookies, 30
    Peanut Butter Gingerbread Men, 36
    Peanut Butter Jumbos, 101
    Peanut Butter Pizza Cookies, 126
    Peanut Butter Raisin Bars, 136
    Peanut Butter Refrigerator Cookies, 212
    Peanut Butter Reindeer, 87
    Peanut Butter Spritz Sandwiches, 118
    Peanut Butter Stars, 171
    Peanut Butter Sugar Cookies, 192
    Peanut Butter Swirl Brownies, 134
Peanut Butter and Chocolate Cookie
    Sandwich Cookies, 116
Peanut Butter Cookies, 122
Peanut Butter Cream Filling, 186
Peanut Butter Jewels, 154

Pecan Caramel Bars, 51
Pecan Crunchies, 214
Pecan Date Bars, 48
Pecan Drops, 181
Pecan Florentines, 76
Pecan Mince Bars, 54
Pecan Turtle Bars, 134
Peppermint Macaroons, 168
Peppermint Refrigerator Slices, 172
Pineapple Almond Shortbread Bars, 224
Pineapple-Oatmeal Cookies, 124
Pineapple Pecan Bars, 139
Pineapple-Raisin Jumbles, 120
Pineapple Topping, 139
Pinecone Cookies, 157
Pinwheel Cookies, 76
Pumpkin Jingle Bars, 219
Pumpkin Pecan Pie Bars, 57

R
Raspberry Almond Sandwich Cookies,
    177
Raspberry Meringue Bars, 139
Refrigerator Cookies
    Choco-Coco Pecan Crisps, 10
    Chocolate-Frosted Lebkuchen, 68
    Chocolate Mint Pinwheels, 106
    Oats 'n' Pumpkin Pinwheels, 80
    Peanut Butter Refrigerator Cookies, 212
    Peppermint Refrigerator Slices, 172
    Pinwheel Cookies, 76
    Slice 'n' Bake Pumpkin Cookies, 18
Rich 'n' Creamy Brownie Bars, 142
Richest Spritz, 91
Rocky Road Brownies, 134
Rum Raisin Balls, 167

S
Sandwich Cookies
    Baked S'Mores, 135
    Chocolate Cookie Sandwiches, 43
    Chocolate Raspberry Linzer Cookies,
        108
    Peanut Butter and Chocolate Cookie
        Sandwich Cookies, 116
    Peanut Butter Spritz Sandwiches, 118
    Raspberry Almond Sandwich Cookies,
        177
    Sandwich Cookies, 203
    Special Chocolate Chip Sandwiches, 156

Sandwich Cookies, *continued*
Walnut Christmas Balls, 29
Santa's Thumbprints, 87
Sesame-Almond Cookies, 125
Shaped Cookies
Almond Melting Moments, 178
Almond-Raspberry Thumbprint
Cookies, 157
Almond Rice Madeleines, 70
Apricot-Pecan Tassies, 14
Bavarian Cookie Wreaths, 19
Brandy Lace Cookies, 66
Butter-Flavored Brickle Drizzles, 206
Candy Shop Pizza, 154
Cherry Coconut Cookies, 184
Cherry Dot Cookies, 164
Cherry Rum Cookies, 174
Cherry Surprises, 150
Cherry Thumbprint Cookies, 172
Choco-Caramel Delights, 79
Chocolate-Caramel Sugar Cookies, 102
Chocolate Cherry Cookies, 40
Chocolate Chip Lollipops, 105
Chocolate Chips Thumbprint Cookies,
98
Chocolate-Dipped Almond Crescents,
80
Chocolate-Dipped Almond Horns, 16,
164
Chocolate-Dipped Brandy Snaps, 176
Chocolate-Dipped Oat Cookies, 79
Chocolate-Gilded Danish Sugar Cones,
146
Chocolate Lace Cornucopias, 114
Chocolate Madeleines, 44
Chocolate Melting Moments, 113
Chocolate Mint Pinwheels, 106
Chocolate Mint Snow-Top Cookies, 109
Chocolate Mint Sugar Cookie Drops,
112
Chocolate Nut Slices, 46
Chocolate Peanut Butter Cups, 182
Chocolate Pistachio Fingers, 72
Chocolate Snow Balls, 203
Chocolate Spritz, 43
Chocolate Sugar Cookies, 102
Chocolate Thumbprints, 186
Cinnamon Pinwheel Cookies, 203
Cookie Pecan Critters, 203
Double Almond Butter Cookies, 25

Shaped Cookies, *continued*
Double Crunch Biscotti, 160
Double Surprise Cookies, 168
Favorite Peanut Butter Cookies, 131
Frosty Cherry Cookies, 163
Giant Oatmeal Cookies, 129
Hidden Treasures, 26
Holiday Almond Wreaths, 89
Holiday Teatime Treats, 153
Honey-Ginger Bourbon Balls, 12
Jam-Filled Chocolate Sugar Cookes, 102
Jingle Jumbles, 22
Kentucky Bourbon Pecan Tarts, 73
Kolacky, 169
Lemon Blossom Cookies, 13
Lemon Pecan Crescents, 173
Lemon Wafers, 24
Lemony Spritz Sticks, 18
Melting Moments, 178
Mini Morsel Meringue Wreaths, 70
Mocha Mint Crisps, 153
New Wave Chocolate Spritz Cookies,
108
No-Bake Peanutty Cookies, 178
Noel Tarts, 167
Norwegian Molasses Cookies, 129
Nutty Chocolate Stars, 117
Orange Sugar Cookies, 121
Peanut Butter Cookies, 122
Peanut Butter Crackles, 22
Peanut Butter Jewels, 154
Peanut Butter Pizza Cookies, 126
Peanut Butter Spritz Sandwiches, 118
Peanut Butter Stars, 171
Pecan Crunchies, 214
Pecan Drops, 181
Richest Spritz, 91
Rum Raisin Balls, 167
Santa's Thumbprints, 87
Sesame-Almond Cookies, 125
Snickerdoodles, 214
Snowballs, 14
Snow-Covered Almond Crescents, 90
Snow Puff Cookies, 163
Soft Spicy Molasses Cookies, 206
Spiced Banana Cookie Wreaths, 90
Spritz Christmas Trees, 171
Spritz Cookies, 17
Sugar Cookie Ornaments, 93
Sugar Cookie Wreaths, 97

Shaped Cookies, *continued*
Toffee Tassies, 183
Triple Chocolate Pretzels, 42
Walnut Christmas Balls, 29
Walnut Jam Crescents, 186
Yuletide Ginger Cookies, 88
Slice 'n' Bake Pumpkin Cookies, 18
Snickerdoodles, 214
Snowballs, 14
Snow Caps, 148
Snow-Covered Almond Crescents, 90
Snow Puff Cookies, 163
Soft Spicy Molasses Cookies, 206
Special Chocolate Chip Sandwiches, 156
Spiced Banana Cookie Wreaths, 90
Spiced Mincemeat Squares, 142
Spicy Gingerbread Cookies, 200
Spicy Pumpkin Cookies, 204
Spritz Christmas Trees, 171
Spritz Cookies, 17
Stained Glass Cookies, 97, 203
Streusel Caramel Bars, 221
Streusel Strawberry Bars, 229
Sugar Cookie Ornaments, 93
Sugar Cookies, 89
Sugar Cookie Wreaths, 97

T
Tinted Frosting, 19
Toffee Tassies, 183
Toffee Topping, 52
Triple Chocolate Cookies, 44
Triple Chocolate Pretzels, 42

U
Ultimate Chocolate Chip Cookies, 211
Ultimate Designer Brownies, 220

V
Vanilla Glaze, 220
Versatile Cutout Cookies, 202

W
Walnut Christmas Balls, 29
Walnut Jam Crescents, 186
White Brownie Bites, 69
White Chocolate Biggies, 100

Y
Yuletide Ginger Cookies, 88

METRIC CONVERSION CHART

VOLUME MEASUREMENTS (dry)

1/8 teaspoon = 0.5 mL
1/4 teaspoon = 1 mL
1/2 teaspoon = 2 mL
3/4 teaspoon = 4 mL
1 teaspoon = 5 mL
1 tablespoon = 15 mL
2 tablespoons = 30 mL
1/4 cup = 60 mL
1/3 cup = 75 mL
1/2 cup = 125 mL
2/3 cup = 150 mL
3/4 cup = 175 mL
1 cup = 250 mL
2 cups = 1 pint = 500 mL
3 cups = 750 mL
4 cups = 1 quart = 1 L

VOLUME MEASUREMENTS (fluid)

1 fluid ounce (2 tablespoons) = 30 mL
4 fluid ounces (1/2 cup) = 125 mL
8 fluid ounces (1 cup) = 250 mL
12 fluid ounces (1 1/2 cups) = 375 mL
16 fluid ounces (2 cups) = 500 mL

WEIGHTS (mass)

1/2 ounce = 15 g
1 ounce = 30 g
3 ounces = 90 g
4 ounces = 120 g
8 ounces = 225 g
10 ounces = 285 g
12 ounces = 360 g
16 ounces = 1 pound = 450 g

DIMENSIONS

1/16 inch = 2 mm
1/8 inch = 3 mm
1/4 inch = 6 mm
1/2 inch = 1.5 cm
3/4 inch = 2 cm
1 inch = 2.5 cm

OVEN TEMPERATURES

250°F = 120°C
275°F = 140°C
300°F = 150°C
325°F = 160°C
350°F = 180°C
375°F = 190°C
400°F = 200°C
425°F = 220°C
450°F = 230°C

BAKING PAN SIZES

Utensil	Size in Inches/Quarts	Metric Volume	Size in Centimeters
Baking or Cake Pan (square or rectangular)	8×8×2	2 L	20×20×5
	9×9×2	2.5 L	22×22×5
	12×8×2	3 L	30×20×5
	13×9×2	3.5 L	33×23×5
Loaf Pan	8×4×3	1.5 L	20×10×7
	9×5×3	2 L	23×13×7
Round Layer Cake Pan	8×1½	1.2 L	20×4
	9×1½	1.5 L	23×4
Pie Plate	8×1¼	750 mL	20×3
	9×1¼	1 L	23×3
Baking Dish or Casserole	1 quart	1 L	—
	1½ quart	1.5 L	—
	2 quart	2 L	—